*Wild Flowers: Where To Gather Them
and How To Preserve Them*

Also, Their Medicinal Uses

by Ward and Lock

with an introduction by Roger Chambers

This work contains material that was originally published in 1861.

*This publication was created and published for the public benefit,
utilizing public funding and is within the Public Domain.*

*This edition is reprinted for educational purposes
and in accordance with all applicable Federal Laws.*

Self Reliance Books

Get more historic titles on animal and stock breeding, gardening and old fashioned skills by visiting us at:

http://selfreliancebooks.blogspot.com/

<h1 style="text-align:center">Introduction</h1>

I am pleased to present yet another title on Ginseng.

The work is in the Public Domain and is re-printed here in accordance with Federal Laws.

As with all reprinted books of this age that are intended to perfectly reproduce the original edition, considerable pains and effort had to be undertaken to correct fading and sometimes outright damage to existing proofs of this title. At times, this task is quite monumental, requiring an almost total "rebuilding" of some pages from digital proofs of multiple copies. Despite this, imperfections still sometimes exist in the final proof and may detract from the visual appearance of the text.

I hope you enjoy reading this book as much as I enjoyed making it available to readers again.

Roger Chambers

PREFACE.

Over meadows—through country lanes—peeping into hedges — can there be anything more delightful than Rambles after Wild Flowers?

> While the bee is humming in the sun,
>   The yellow cowslip springs;
> And hark! from yonder woodland's side
>   Again the cuckoo sings!

It is the purpose of this little Handy Book to point out the most beautiful haunts of these " darlings of the woods and hedges "—to describe their habits, forms, and uses,—and, through them, to awaken in the mind a love of the Beautiful.

We shall also show how Wild Flowers may be successfully cultivated in Windows and Town Gardens, and thus present us at all seasons with the best assemblage of beautiful and interesting forms, either of single plants or well-massed groups.

PREFACE.

Our labours in this delightful pursuit have furnished us with some little wisdom as to the growth of Wild Flowers in gardens and windows, and their capabilities of adding to the beauty of the parterre or border, as well as interesting the grower with all manner of suggestions.

> "Sweet nurslings of the vernal skies,
>   Bathed in soft airs, and fed with dew,
> What more than magic in you lies,
>   To fill the heart's fond view!
> In childhood's sports, companions gay;
>   In sorrow, on life's downward way,
> How soothing! in our last decay,
>   Memorials prompt and true."

HANDY BOOK

OF

WILD FLOWERS.

JANUARY.

ALL things are very still, methinks, and quiet,
Insects are sleeping, and beneath the cold earth
Are seeds unnumber'd, waiting for the summer,
That calls them forth.   A few frail, friendly plants,
Withstand all storms, and, e'en in this dull month,
Look green and cheerful.

LET us go into the fields, for January will soon give place to her sister, February: she has already wakened up her sleeping flowers, harbingers of lengthened days, and the coming back of punctual birds, and bade the hazel to hang forth her tassels in sheltered places.   Leaves of the wild Honeysuckle began to open nearly a week since, but now they are fully expanded among the brakes, and present a cheerful contrast to leafless branches, or dark green bushes of wild juniper.

It is cheering to look upon their young green tints, to think that in the course of a few short weeks the dull and cheerless landscape will be reclothed with beauty—that the leafless shrubs and trees will blossom and look green, and that where not a sound is heard, except the sighing of the wind or the rushing of some wayside stream, glad songs of singing birds will resound from every bush, with the bleating of sheep, and insects' hum of joy.

B

Did you hear the voice of one who spoke from out the hedge-bank? It was a small grasshopper, awakened from his winter sleep. The bright warm sunbeams of this unusually mild morning has caused his weak voice to be heard.

The garland which botanists have woven whereby to adorn the brow of January is but slender. Stillingfleet, in his Calendar of Flora, speaks of six different flowers as pertaining to this dull month. But changes have taken place since then; and botanists of the present time refer to the snowdrop (*Galanthus nivalis*), and the daisy (*Bellis perennis*), to a somewhat later period. True it is, that the peeping forth of the first from her green hood, and the expanding of the "wee, modest, crimson-tipped flower," depends on the mildness of the season. The Snowdrop, or Fair Maid of February, may be seen by chance in sheltered places, beside streams, at the end of January; but she pretends by right to the month whose name she bears; the daisy, too, rarely expands till March; a child is she of blustering winds and hurrying showers, yet most unlike her parents, meekly smiling from amid the turf, and seeming to propitiate the racking clouds when they hurry athwart the heavens.

Surely the Common Chickweed (*Stellaria media*) groweth everywhere, and at all seasons, except when the ground is hard frozen, or covered deep with snow. She belongs, therefore, to January, and may be numbered among the small flowers which this month calls forth, with little of outward beauty to commend them, and yet wonderfully adapted for their place in the creation.

The common chickweed has many sisters, and of these some are found in meadows and hedge-banks, or in thickets; others on the banks of mountain streams; others again on high hills; but the common chickweed grows everywhere— by streams, in meadows, on heaps of rubbish, or sandy places, where most other plants refuse to vegetate.

Old Gerard wrote concerning this plant in his time, and notices her dissimilar localities. "The common chickweed," said he, in his quaint way, "rises up with stalks a cubit high, and sometimes higher, yet oft-times she almost creepeth upon the ground. A great many stalks spring from one root, long, and round, and slender, full of joints, with a couple of leaves growing out of every knot or joint, of a light green colour. The stalks are something cleare, and as it were transparent, or thorow-shining; and about the joints they may be oftentimes of a very light red colour, as be those of pellitorie of the wall; the floures be whitish on the top, like the floures of stitchwort, but yet lesser, in whose places succeed long knops, but not great, wherein the seed is contained."

Such is the description given by Gerard when he looked upon this invaluable plant, growing, it might be, in his garden at Nantwich, in Cheshire, during the reign of Henry VIII., or beside the river Weever, where he loved to wander in his boyhood days, searching for wild plants, and taking notes of their wonderful construction. He speaks of the long knops wherein seed is contained, and no part of this wild plant is more worthy of remark, either in their perfect condition or when advancing to maturity.

Observe the variety which, even at this dull season, the whole plant presents. One might almost fancy that she had within her some magic power whereby to concentrate the developments of different seasons. One small branch is covered with green leaves; another presents a bud in different stages of verdure, or of decay; a third upholds a white star-like blossom to the sun; a fourth is covered with four-sided and light-green capsules; and, lastly, in some, the stalk has assumed a curved form, and the seed-vessels bend towards the earth. And why is this? Because the chickweed grows frequently on high walls, or in places exposed to fierce winds and driving showers; a peculiar provision is consequently required for the protection of the seeds. Observe, therefore, a small penthouse formed by the capsule, for the capsule in this plant is permanent, and does not wither and fall off like those of the poppy or cornflower; neither does it always stand upright, but becomes reversed at an appointed season and during a few days, at the end of which the stem gradually straightens, and the seed-vessel is presented to the influence of whatever wandering sunbeams may find their way among the clouds. Again, another expedient becomes developed; the seed-vessel, acted on by the elements of air and light, opens into six small divisions at the top, through which the same elements find a ready entrance. These have an allotted ministry to fulfil; they cause the seeds to ripen; and when this process is completed, the stem bends again, and empties, as from an urn, innumerable seeds upon the earth.

Thus does every single stem change its position at least four times, and each for a definite object. Upright, when first the leaves expand, and the small white flower begins to open, with its tiny, mirror-like petals, so arranged as to catch and reflect every ray of light. Bending, when the perfecting of the seed seems to require a downward position; for, as the chickweed grows most commonly on walls or rocks, or heaps of rubbish, amid places where little moisture can be imbibed by the roots, it is essential that every facility should be given, in order that its vessels may absorb whatever evaporation may result from heavy rains or night dews. But when the seeds are fully grown, and sunbeams are required for their ripening, the stem gradually straightens, and the heavy-laden seed-vessel is held up to their full influence. Thus it continues till the process of ripening is effected; and then, gradually resuming its downward position, the seeds, as already mentioned, are scattered to the earth.

Poets of old times gathered much from nature. They derived from that inexhaustible source many of their happiest suggestions. Who can look upon the light-green and gracefully-moulded seed-vessel of the chickweed, without recalling to mind the cornucopia, full to overflowing with the richest productions of Flora and Pomona? or the urn-shaped capsule of the common poppy, without remembering the Roman urn? In like manner, Callimachus is said to have taken his idea of the Corinthian capital from a basket of toys, which had been left on the tomb of a young lady, and became entwined with leaves of the classic acanthus; and Gothic sculptors adopted those of the *Acanthus spinosus* as one of their choicest ornaments.

Examine a small seed contained in the capsule of the common chickweed, concerning which old Gerard remarks, "that little birds in cages, especially linnets, are refreshed therewith, when they loathe their meat; whereupon it is called by some *Passerina.*"

And not only are small birds in cages refreshed by those small brown and thickly-coated seeds, which enwrap within them the rudiments of innumerable plants; but they present a continual repast to such wayfaring birds as remain stationary throughout the winter. And if it be allowable to repeat in spirit, if not in words, thoughts which arose within me when observing the wonderful construction of the common chickweed during this chill month, I would remark that its native character remains unchanged either by soil or climate—a modest-looking flower, which few might care to look upon if they had not learned somewhat concerning its beauty and its worth, and how the hand of Him who made it has impressed upon its pale-green leaves characters which those who love to hear and speak of Him may read, and which, in reading, will make their hearts glow within them! What sees the stranger in passing by? A small

and insignificant-looking weed, covering the top of an old
wall, or springing from interstices where the mortar has
fallen out between the stones. What sees the botanist in
this simple weed? An object of great interest; formed
especially for the place which it is designed to fill; a memento
of the care of its Creator; and not for the plant only, but
for a brotherhood of birds which depend upon the ripening
of its seeds for their support.

> There grows not, there blooms not, on mountain, rock, or wall,
> A choicer flower than this, which men the chickweed call.
> A weed for chicken truly, for "little birdies" too,
> Who trust their Maker's bounty, the dreary winter through.
>
> Look on that chickweed, mourner, and list the grateful strain,
> Of her who sings to praise Him, 'mid driving wind and rain.
> That warbling creature hath not, nor fields nor hoarded corn,
> And yet she sweetly singeth the leafless boughs among.
> Her clear voice is telling from out the lonely tree,
> That He who feeds the lone one, doth surely care for thee.
>
> Her plumes are rudely ruffled, the day is nearly gone,
> But she heeds not, she fears not, and still she singeth on :
> O weep not thus, poor mourner! the storm shall pass away;
> For me sweet spring is coming, for thee a brighter day.

The Groundsel (*Senecio vulgaris*), expands also in sheltered
places when the air is mild; but rather by permission of
sunny gleams, and soft south winds, than as actually belonging to the month. Who has not felt even in icy January
one of those sudden changes in the weather which unbind
the frozen streams, and cause the snow to melt rapidly?
Evanescent indeed they are, scarcely felt than vanishing,
and oftentimes succeeded by a greater degree of cold, but
during their brief stay causing the chickweed and groundsel
to look green, and open their tiny flowers, and the archangel
to appear on hedge-banks.

The Archangel (*Lamium album*), which thrives best in
places where every blade of grass serves as a conduit for the

rain, telleth her own tale. It is one that the passer-by will do well to hear, for scarcely throughout the vegetable kingdom does a more beautiful adaptation of form and structure to adverse circumstances anywhere exist. The stem is angular, and consequently well adapted to its windy location; the upper lip is entire and vaulted, and forms a canopy over the otherwise defenceless seeds, by means of which they are defended from the rain. And not unfrequently does the red Dead-Nettle grow beside its statelier relative, an humble weed, yet worthy of close inspection. Much, too, of exquisite finishing is obvious in its six delicately-tinted flowers, which surround the stems in a double row. And over the small defenceless seeds bend also canopies designed to protect them from the wet. The chaffinch seeks for this welcome plant, his quick eye discovers it among the dripping grass, and he speedily deflorates entire whorls of its early crimson blossoms, while feeding on the unripe seeds.

The herb Robert (*Geranium Robertianum*) sheds a pleasant fragrance in its growing-place, and recalls to mind a celebrated naturalist of the Oxford Botanic Garden. The leaves when green are the haunt and home of a pretty little parasite, the *Dothidea Robertiana*: her dwelling is scattered with innumerable others, in minute dot-like hemispherical black spots, with nothing of outward symmetry to commend them; but when submitted to a magnifier, they appear highly wrought, and well adapted for the dwelling-place of their occupant.

FEBRUARY.

" Now mountain snows dissolve against the sun,
And streams yet new from precipices run.
E'en in this early dawning of the year,
They bring the plough, and yoke the sturdy steer."
                                        GEORGICS.

FAIREST among flowers are the " Maids of February,"
(*Galanthus nivalis*,) which peep from out their light-green
vests, in troops along the streamlet's brink. Who does not
hail their coming up in this changing month, when snows
are melting from the fields, and a soft spring-like breeze
oft-times succeeds to the cold east wind? It is pleasant to
go abroad after a tedious confinement to the house, to watch
the driving clouds chasing one the other across the vault of
heaven, alternating in their fleeting shadows with the sunbeams that break forth at intervals, and brighten the landscape with a rapid radiance. Make the most of such glad
days, for they pass too quickly; and though the air is balmy,
and wreathing mists rest at times upon the hills, many
cheerless hours must intervene before the woods are covered
with leaves and the meadows look bright with flowers.

But we will not think of such unwelcome changes.
February is in her mildest mood, and the song-thrush, the
blackbird, and the raven, begin to build their nests. The
two former wisely select an evergreen-bush or retired
thicket, where the blossoms of the alder and the hazel begin
to open, and leaves of the wild gooseberry and currant to
expand; the latter, who regards neither the rough east
wind nor the drifting snow, chooses the leafless branches of
some high tree for " the cradle of his callow brood," and
may be seen wheeling in his sportive flight, amid the
utmost rigours of the season.

Truly this changing month is equally bitter and inconstant; at one time gladdening the heart with bright hopes and the thought of much that is verdurous and joyful; at another, driving her snow-drifts and flakes against the traveller, and causing furious gusts of wind to sweep across the hills.

But whether thus pitiless or relenting, the Fair Maid of February punctually awaits her bidding. It may be that a fierce drifting wind eddies the snow in heaps around her, or else that some wandering sunbeam, which has struggled through the clouds, tinges her meek pale forehead with somewhat of a golden hue; while the throstle and the blackbird bid welcome to the sunny gleam, and body forth such joyous notes as man, with all his boasted powers, cannot imitate. February has called for her; and forth she comes from out the damp cold earth, throwing aside her green hood, and looking on the dripping mosses, and the wayside streamlet as it goes sounding through the dell.

How beautiful are such small sisterhoods of peerless flowers! and who does not love the Snowdrop, that herald of the spring, which in her first perfect beauty pertains exclusively to the month whose name she bears? Methinks a voice is heard, soft, yet clear, speaking from amid those snow-white sisters, keeping time with the music of yonder unfrozen stream, and bidding all to be of good cheer, for that the driving gale and storms of sleet will soon pass by, and that spring is surely on her way. I remember, as if it were but yesterday, that frequently when a child I used to run into the garden to see if the snowdrops were come up, whenever the cold east wind began to lull, and the snow to melt in patches among the hollows of our bleak hills. Often, too, in our pleasant village, did the children run merrily to the entrance of a neighbouring glen, where steep acclivities, covered with brushwood, guarded a bright stream that was rarely frozen, and where a colony of snowdrops re-assembled from year to year along the margin. They loved the snowdrops as if they were their own small sisters ; and joyfully would they come bounding back to tell their mothers that the winter would soon be over, because the snowdrops were come.

In sheltered places, also, flowers of the Common and Dwarf Elder (*Sambucus ebulus* and *nigra*) begin to open. The first derives a name *sambuca*, an ancient musical instrument in much use among the Romans. At the present day, Italian peasants construct a simple pipe, which they call *sampogna*, from the tough branches of this plant. Somewhat of sadness is associated with the Dwarf Elder, or Danewort, a plant of stunted growth, and which is found most commonly among rubbish and the ruined foundations of old buildings. Those who visit the deserted walls of Selborne Priory in quest of plants, may find the dwarf elder among its ruins. Those, too, who like to moralise on the evanescent nature of worldly greatness, and to contrast its mutability with the permanency of nature, when looking on the clear prattling stream that flows amid woods and meadows, as once it flowed in the days of John, may not dislike to be reminded that Selborne Priory was founded by Peter de la Roche, or Rupidus, one of those enterprising foreigners who resorted to the court of King John, and who afterwards became Lord Chief Justiciary of England, and Bishop of Winchester, as also a kind of viceroy, on whom devolved the civil affairs of England.

The life of De Rupidus was one of varied and romantic incidents ; at one time equally renowned for his benefactions and vast powers ; at another, distrusted by the confederate barons ; and withdrawing to the Holy Land, where he devoted all his wealth and energies to checking the encroachments of the infidels. At length, wearied with a life of adventure, and longing to revisit his native land, he returned to England in the beginning of the thirteenth century, and commenced building the Priory of Selborne, in a beautiful and retired place, midway between Winchester and Farnham.

The celebrated natural historian of Selborne speaks of the dwarf elder as growing among the rubbish and ruined foundations of the Priory. He notices, also, other rare plants which are found in its locality, and which most commonly blossom in this month. Among such, the *Helleborus fœtidus*, or Bear's-foot, grows profusely all over the high wood, and Coney-croft-hanger. Different species flower richly under the shade of trees, and expand their singular blossoms in even the most sterile season; hence their garden relatives, the Christmas Rose (*Helleborus niger*), which is supposed to be the real black hellebore of the ancients, is often gathered for winter bouquets, at the same time with the holly. Young children go trooping forth to the sterile haunts of such as pertain to Britain; oft-times on rocky banks, beneath which some streamlet is suspended in its rapid course by the magic power of frost; and beautiful is the effect produced by the polished leaves and red berries of numerous holly-bushes peeping from amid their snowy coverings! while beneath them spread the pale-green yellow flowers of the *Helleborus viridus*. This plant is also noticed by White, in his "History of Selborne," as common in a deep stony lane turning to Norton Farm; he mentions that it dies down to the ground early in autumn, and springs up again about February, flowering almost as soon as it reappears.

Spots of equal interest with that of Selborne might be cited as favourite haunts of the dwarf elder. It grows profusely near Carisbrook Castle, in the Isle of Wight; below the time-worn walls of Scarborough Castle; beside the old Roman Watling-street road, where it is crossed by the footpath from Norton to Wilton, in Northamptonshire;—places of deep historic interest, and associating with the danewort or dwarf elder, thrilling remembrances of past days.

The Common Elder, on the contrary, is blended with homesteads in the country, and many a pleasant thought of rural walks and occupations. True it is that, being frequently bird-sown, or planted by the wind—that random sower—on walls or lofty towers, or the trunks of decaying trees, the common elder may be seen occasionally among the ruins of deserted homes, yet, still with an air of cheerfulness. But more commonly this well-known plant grows profusely in farmyards, where its white and scented blossoms shade the gable-end of some old dwelling-house, or droop over the dark pool, which is tenanted by ducks and geese, and forms the favourite resort of cows in sultry weather.

The Elder is applied to important multifarious uses. Its berries supply a favourite home-made wine; the leaves are valued by the farmer for driving mice away from granaries, and moles from their usual haunts; and the pith, on account of its lightness, is used for small toys, and electric purposes. A decoction of the leaves also destroys such aphides as infest delicate plants; and the roots form an ingredient in dyeing black. The botanist finds in this plant an object of considerable interest; for if a twig is partially cut, then cautiously broken, and the divided portions are carefully drawn asunder, the spiral air-vessels, resembling a screw, may be distinctly seen. The angler prefers its tough and yellow wood for the top of his angling-rod; and the fisherman for needles wherewith to weave his nets. And those whose attention is directed to the geography of plants, observe in this species a singular adaptation to almost every locality and soil; while the dwarf elder has a restricted growth, and was unknown in Devonshire till the autumn of 1827, when it was discovered by the side of the new road from Shalton to St. Mary's Church, a few hundred yards only from the latter place, and still nearer to the guide-post; where likewise grew the *Rumex acutus, var. sanguineus*, or blood-veined dock, of which the leaves, veined with a crimson juice, present a singular and beautiful appearance.

The ground had, doubtless, been thrown up from a considerable depth, and seeds, buried perhaps for ages, were suddenly exposed to the influence of air and light. The elder, therefore, obtained a growing-place where hitherto it had been unknown. And most welcome is this tree in exposed situations—a friendly tree, which shelters all of lesser growth, and fosters many a weakly scion, though, perchance, that scion has been sown by a tempest, and is destined, with its brethren, to renew the honours of the forest. The elder also quickly forms a hedge in moist places, and often presents much of Sylvan beauty in marsh lands.

Conspicuous among leafless hedges are the drooping catkins of the Hazel-nut tree (*Coryllus avellana*), with their vivid crimson styles.   That tree, invaluable to the shepherd, forms his choicest hurdles for penning sheep; the angler regards it with peculiar interest; the painter, too, often introduces the hazel on quarry banks, when painting forest scenery; and the botanist visits its wild habitats in quest of his favourite plants.   Evelyn, who loved the wild hazel, speaks of it as affecting barren ground, especially quarries, and associates it with those of Hasebury in Wiltshire, Haselingfield in Cambridgeshire, and Haselmere in Surrey.   Who that ever visited those wild spots, where the labours of men have ceased, and Nature has re-assumed her empire, can forget their beauty and their loneliness, and the effect produced by huge lichen-dotted stones among giant hazels, of which the tangled roots sustain, at intervals, masses of sandy soil, intermixed with pebbles, beneath which the wild rabbit forms her burrow, and early ferns begin to unfold their light-green leaves!   Among those quarries not a sound is heard in February, except the murmurs of gusty winds; but the air is fresh, and magnificent masses of rock-shaped clouds assemble on the ridges of those old quarries, which seem resting from their past labours in primeval stillness.

But the Daisy (*Bellis perennis*) grows there profusely, companion of the gusty wind, and smiling on the storm-clouds that chase each other in their fitful moods.   If the old quarries awake remembrances of by-gone days, and cause him who wanders among them to feel as if utterly

alone, so wild and desolate, yet richly garnished with
natural beauties are they, the daisy awakens far different
feelings. That bonny gem, the "wee modest crimson-
tipped flower," recalls many a going forth to gather flowers
in the meadow, or by the streamlet brink, where grew
small colonies, in their distinctiveness. But wherefore they

thus grew apart from one another, forming as it were small
households, is a problem which even Linnæus would be un-
able to solve.

Examine the daisy narrowly; it will reward your trouble.
Turn this robin among flowers in all directions, and on every
side you will discover some new beauty. The petals are
snow-white; they form a striking contrast to the golden
tufts of tubular florets in the centre, and are backed by a
delicate star-like calyx tipped with bright crimson. All
this is obvious; but, were it possible to examine the exquisite internal machinery by which the beauty of the daisy
is developed and sustained, and its various movements are
effected, what care, what skill, would be discovered! for
the daisy not only shuts its pinky lashes at night, but care-

fully folds them over the yellow disk when storms are abroad. The effect is particularly obvious: in meadow land, where the daisy grows luxuriantly among short herbage, that meadow, during one part of the day, seems covered with a white sheet; at another, not a daisy is to be seen, if, perchance, a shower wheels its course athwart the heavens. And how singular is the fact, that the facility for thus defending the stamens and anthers from a humid atmosphere is peculiar to such plants as inhabit a fickle climate!

The daisy was Chaucer's favourite flower; and he loved it even to old age, with all the enthusiasm of his boyhood days. He tells us, in his own unrivalled poetry, that he had risen repeatedly in the grey of morning, and watched beside a tuft of daisies, to see them gradually expand; and that at eveningtide he knelt beside the same peerless flowers, to watch the closing of their starry rims. The daisy could alone allure him from his study and his books; and, heedless of the stirring times in which he lived, the venerable father of English poetry, having exhausted all the powers of poetic fervour in its praise, would seem to to derive fresh inspiration from his favourite flower as he exclaimed, "Oh, the daisy, it is sweet!" He called it the "eye of the day;" and throughout all time this unassuming flower ought to be associated with his name:

> " Of all the flowres in the mede
> Than love I most these flowres of white and rede;
> Such that men call daisies in our town;
> To them I have so great affection,
> That I get up, and walking in the mede
> To seen this flowre agenst the sunne spreade:
> When it upriseth early by the morrow,
> That blissful sight softeneth my sorrow.
> And when that eve come on, I renne blithe,
> As soon as ever the sunne ginneth west,
> To seen this flowre, how it will go to reste."
>
> CHAUCER.

MARCH.

There is something of gentleness in thy nature, stern, blustering March, else surely even a few wild flowers would not welcome thee.

YEARS have passed since I stood looking with childish curiosity at an old ruin, amid woods and rocky banks in a quiet little valley, remote from any public road. Gable-ends and a large oriel, with an iron-bossed door, opening into a large hall, told somewhat of its past history. An armorial shield too was conspicuous on the front of the old grey porch, but so time-worn and lichen-dotted, that no one could decipher aught respecting it : and the history of those who once dwelt within that dilapidated ruin was wrapt in impenetrable obscurity. Great they might have been on earth ; a race distinguished, perchance, for talents and bold daring ; but no memorial remains to soothe ancestral pride, or stimulate to equal deeds. They lived, and are forgotten ; and the old house, their home—the home it might be of successive generations—presented, when last I saw it, bare walls, and roofless chambers, and broken pavements, through which the dock and dandelion looked forth on the surrounding desolation.

I loved that spot from my earliest childhood, because, although exceeding desolate, it was associated with sunny days and pleasant rambles. I loved it, too, because, in one spot, beside the margin of an ample stream that murmured through the valley, grew tall Butterburs, or Long-stalked Coltsfoot (*Tussilago petasites*), which herald, in their early flowering, the coming back of the migratory dove, whose soft cooings were heard in that wild spot.

The colony of butterburs occupied a sunny nook, guarded with high, rocky banks, and sloping to the water's edge ; they grew there profusely, isolated as regards their growing-place, because unknown elsewhere, but numerous in their companionship. The small and purplish flowers had little of external beauty, but the leaves were equally unique and interesting. The grew to the height of five or six feet, and being excessively large and hollowed, like umbrellas, they were carried in triumph by the village children. You might often see a company of these joyous urchins, when gossiping and laughing among the ruins, and searching for

bright yellow dandelions and chickweeds, driven to take shelter beneath the friendly leaves of the butterburs. Those broad leaves mounted on strong foot-stalks formed a kind of grove, from which ever and anon some fearless urchin would dart forth with a leaf carried in triumph above his head; and as often his little sister, peeping from beneath these umbrellas of Nature's making, would urge him to come back, while the rain streamed from off his leaf, and he stood as if in defiance, watching the heavy rain-drops as they fell upon the surface of the stream. Then what delight was there among the younglings, when in a moment the leaf gave way, and the boastful urchin rushed back to his young companions, dripping wet, and half ashamed of his adventure !

That same quiet nook was the scene of many a joyous gathering of young children, and the more heavily it rained the more did they rejoice; many a half-serious and half-comic face looked forth at the driving storm, wishing that it would continue, and thus afford a good pretext for playing truant a little longer.

But this was only on a holiday ; and when the rain began to fall at other times, the same small grove of butterburs was resorted to by sheep and poultry, who found a dry and comfortable place of shelter beneath the leaves. It seemed as if those hospitable butterburs had much to offer; for bees, in sunny weather, might be seen busily employed among the flowers; and winged insects of all kinds resorted thither. Their early flowering, and sweet nectareous juice, caused them in old times to be planted beside hives; but the custom has been laid aside because of their rapid increase and penetrating roots, which render it difficult to exterminate them.

The Common Coltsfoot (*Tussilago farfara*) grew there also, but not in the same locality. Their more stately brethren occupied a sheltered nook, but they were content to vegetate on a heap of rubbish near the ruin, spreading their broad leaves among the stones, and throwing up innumerable yellow flowers. This plant, the first to vegetate in marl or limestone, also affects moist and clayey soil; the roots spread with incredible rapidity, and the smallest portion, though buried to the depth of a yard, rapidly sends up a stem to the surface. The generic name, derived from *tussis*, a cough, denotes its admirable qualities in allaying pectoral disorders; and Pliny mentions that in his time it was much used for smoking, as a remedy for obstinate coughs, and also to assist asthmatic persons. The white and cottony under-surface of the leaves, when wrapped in linen, and dipped in a solution of saltpetre, and dried in the sun, make the best tinder, and the leaves form the basis of the British herb tobacco.

Such are the various uses of this unassuming plant, which renders cheerful many a solitary and sterile spot, and affords a valuable medicine to the neighbouring cottager.

Few plants produce a better effect for landscape fore-grounds than the common coltsfoot. Magnificent and broad effects of light, with sharp decided touches of shadow, are readily produced; whilst the exquisite rich reddish green of their velvet-looking leaves gives a peculiar fresh-ness and vigour to the foreground, when judiciously ar-ranged. Few plants are equal to the coltsfoot in this respect; and artists who desire to obtain a striking effect in their foregrounds will do well to visit the growing-places of this common plant, and to study in all their varieties the effects of light and shade, especially towards evening, when the sun often sheds a partial, yet broad gleam of light, over the fading landscape.

I remember the old ruin in connection with one of Salvator Rosa's inimitable pictures, wherein the deep dark shade of a near rock threw off in bold relief a group of dancing peasants, upon whom the sun shone brightly. Thus it was with the time-worn pile. Though grey, and lichen-dotted, crowded with elder bushes and partially mantled with ivy, its tall gable-ends were seen from afar when brightened by the sun-beams that warmed many a wild flower into leaf and beauty, even before the appointed time of its appearing. The place was also exceedingly fragrant, for Mezereons grew there profusely,

> " Though leafless, well attired, and thick beset
> With blushing leaves investing every spray."

Examine the buds of this fragrant plant, the Spurge Olive, or Dwarf-Bay, (*Daphne mezereum;*) for not only may the flowers, but even the stamens and anthers, be distinctly seen, and that a considerable time before they unfold. Thus wonderfully prepared for their development, the beautiful red flowers appear even in this changing month, and often betray the parent tree by their sweet scent, though concealed in a thorny brake. Such an empurpled and perfumed branch, brought to the bedside of Mrs. Tighe, inspired her muse when the lamp of life burned feebly :—

> " Odours of spring, my sense ye charm,
>   With fragrance premature ;
> And 'mid these days of sad alarm,
>   Almost to hope allure.
>
> Methinks with purpose soft ye come,
>   To tell of brighter hours ;
> Of May's blue skies, abundant bloom,
>   Her sunny gales and showers."

And yet, though beautiful among flowers—attractive too, because of its exceeding fragrance—beware of the bright red berries. No one may taste them with impunity ; six of the berries will destroy a wolf ; but, strange to say, they are acceptable to different kinds of singing birds, finches especially, who eat the roots of the wild arum.

The Spurge Laurel (*D. laureola*) loved the same wild spot. This pleasing shrub bears at the summit of its branchless stem tufts of spreading, bright-green, and shiny leaves, and being hardy, and of ready growth, forms a stock whereon to graft the more ornamental species. The flowers diffuse a grateful scent, especially in an evening, and are acceptable to those who delight in floreal perfumes. The ripe black berries are eagerly resorted to by small birds that frequent sheltered places. Many such sung sweetly beside the old grey ruin ; you might hear them in the early morning, and late at evening, pouring forth their symphony of mingled notes—some loud and deep ; others sweet and inward ; others, again, with a full gush of melody, making the heart glad, and shaming those who had no thought of thankfulness.

I have said that children frequented that solitary place. One of their chief attractions consisted in the rich carpeting of Dandelions that sprung up through the interstices of the broken pavement. This plant (*Leontodon taraxacum*), though mentioned by different botanists as flowering in April, opened its yellow blossoms towards the end of March; for the place was warm and sheltered, and ivy-covered walls served to keep off the fierce east wind when it swept in hollow gusts through the valley. Children, therefore, sought for them in spring, when they looked like golden stars shining among green leaves; and when in autumn their beautiful seeds formed globes of down:—

> " Dandelion, with globe of down,
> The school-boy's clock in every town:
> While the truant puffs amain,
> To conjure lost hours back again."

The generic name is derived from two Greek words— signifying a lion—and a tooth, on account of its jagged leaves. I have often looked with admiration on those leaves, and contrasted their formation with such as pertain to the butterbur; the one singularly adapted for the admission of rain and heavy dew; the other designed to keep the roots dry. The reason for this difference may be readily explained: the butterbur generally grows beside streams; the dandelion in dry and stony places.

Some persons affect to despise this brilliant yet humble plant. " The dandelion," say they, " grows everywhere; on road-sides, and heaps of rubbish; it springs up through the interstices of broken pavements, and is associated with poverty and desolation." And what more beautiful than to become the friend of those whom every one forsakes? The gaudy train of exotic flowers, and the rose, the garden's queen, speedily desert the neglected garden; exotic creepers that entwined, it may be, some richly-sculptured temple, or flung their cluster of fragrant blossoms around the painted window, disappear with the prosperity to which they owe their birth. It is otherwise with the friendly dandelion. When carriage-wheels are heard no longer in the deserted court, and the great hall-door is closed for the last time, it seems as if the dandelion watched in her hiding-place for some fissure in the pavement; and when this occurs, her green head presently emerges, and her bright joyous flowers look forth, making cheerful the lonely place from which all else of beauty has departed.

The dandelion grows also beside many a cottage-door, on lone heaths, where the soil is stony, and the good cottager vainly seeks to cover the old porch with a wild clematis, or the dog-rose, or wild honeysuckle. She even mounts the thatched roof, and strikes her root into the thatch beside the stonecrop or sengreen; but neither the stonecrop, nor yet the sengreen, flower thus early; the dandelion alone expands her broad yellow disk, watching the progress of the sun, and closing early in the afternoon. Children are uniformly attracted with bright colours; and hence, perchance, the pleasure which they took in visiting the old ruin—for nowhere else was such a luxuriant carpeting of green leaves and flowers to be seen. They often made an humble imitation of Pandean pipes with the hollow flower-stalks fitted one into the other, wherewith to set their young companions dancing; strange mimicry, it seemed, of the minstrel strain and courtly festivities, that, if we deem aright, were heard and seen within the spacious area where grew those humble dandelions.

The globular white head of this favourite flower, when seen in autumn, was also eagerly sought after; and happy was the urchin, who, with one full deep-drawn breath could send the arrow-shaped seeds floating on the air. I have often watched the performance of this feat; and while his playmates looked on and wondered, I have pleased myself with noticing the fairy-formed arrows as they poised themselves in their rapid flight, and after being carried hither and thither according to the currents of even a slight breeze, they dropped one by one upon the earth, from whence they emerge in spring with leaves and flowers wherewith to gladden, it may be, some otherwise cheerless growing-place.

And as regards the many valuable qualities assigned to this offspring of blustering March, I may briefly notice that the roots, when roasted, are a good substitute for coffee, for which purpose they are especially cultivated along the banks of the Rhine; and that when a swarm of locusts had destroyed the harvest in the island of Minorca, many of the inhabitants subsisted on this plant.

In one spot beside the margin of the stream, where grew the butterburs, an elegant Rose-Willow (*Salix Helix*) was seen drooping above the water. This tree also was a favourite resort of children; its smooth and polished twigs, of a pale yellowish or purple ash colour, with young green leaves, presented a pleasing contrast to its pendent catkins, and as the branches drooped within the reach of our younger neighbours, many a small basket was made from its long slender and flexible shoots for holding fruit or flowers. Bees, too, how they loved that tree! On sunny days in March you might almost fancy that a swarm had alighted on the topmost branches, so pleasant was the humming sound of those industrious creatures, who worked while the urchins played beneath, and set them an example of quiet cheerfulness and industry.

Lessons, indeed, of cheerfulness right merrily did the urchins con, but they cared little for those of industry on a summer holiday. Why, indeed, should they? The wisest of men has said, "there is a time for all things—a time to play, and a time to work;" and never, except on holidays, might those same urchins resort to their favourite spot. When there, however, they greatly rejoiced in their liberty, and their hearty laughs and merry voices made the valley ring. You might see them in all directions, some playing at hide-and-seek among the bushes, some even weaving their pretty baskets with twigs of the rose-willow; others seeking for such wild flowers as open warily in March, though rather pertaining to the sunbeams and showers of April. Among these, the Lesser Celandine (*Ranunculus ficaria*), with its bright yellow and glossy enamelled petals, the herald of a joyous train, especially delighted them; but still more sweet-scented and hairy Violets, (*V. odorata* and *Viola hirta*) were rejoiced in when found. They grew on a sunny hazel bank, with occasionally flesh-coloured or white varieties; and softly on memory's ear fall the notes of a simple song, sung by one of the village children in reference to this favourite flower, that may be echoed by many hearts wedded to the charms of nature :—

> " She lifts up her dewy eye of blue,
> To the younger sky of the self-same hue:
> And when the spring comes with her host
> Of flowers, that flower belov'd the most
> Shrinks from the crowd, that may confuse
> Her heavenly odours, and virgin hues.
> The morning star of all the flowers,
> The pledge of daylight's lengthened hours;
> Oh ! 'mid the roses ne'er forget,
> The beauteous virgin violet !"

APRIL.

> Oh! the spring, the spring-like feeling,
>   When soft the south winds blow;
> And from glens and heather stealing,
>   Melts silently the snow.
>
> When the stream, from the old spout springing,
>   Has burst her icy chain;
> And the titlark, sweetly singing,
>   Tells of flowers and leaves again.

APRIL is the youth and spring-tide of the year. The Hawthorn and the Willow begin to bud; and the herb Robert, and White Champion, beautify the places of their growth: the one, which derives its name from a celebrated curator of the Oxford Botanic Garden, grows on hedge-banks, or on walls, and heaps of rubbish; the other, heralding the cuckoo, and oft-times so plentiful in meadows and fallow-fields as to make them appear quite white, is found occasionally with double blossoms. With them come trooping a goodly assemblage of flowers, verging either on the past month, or else welcoming such of their beauteous sisters as pertain to May, or intermediate between both—yet generally known, as regards their time of flowering, by the brightness of their hues; for pale colours pertain to the earliest flowers, and richer tints to those which greet the ardent beams of the sun, when he rises high in the heavens.

The *Oxalis acetosella*, or Wood-Sorrel, is found in woods and shady hedges, and on heaths, where its beautiful white petals are often seen in contrast with deep green mosses, and as frequently beside some clear streamlet, when leaping from out a rocky bank, beside which are ferns and flowers, crowding and thronging, and damp with the glistening spray. The wood-sorrel is a general favourite, the more especially because its place of growth is ever amid scenes to which the mind recurs with unwearied delight; and where, perchance, some of childhood's happiest hours have passed swiftly, in an April holiday, when tasks were fitly done, and books were put aside, and young enthusiasts went forth in all their gladness to listen for the "cuckoo's one word spoken," or to seek for their favourite flower in places where its familiar face has looked forth from year to year.

This small plant has an important station among her sisters in wood or field. An infusion of the leaves affords a refreshing liquor in ardent fevers, and when boiled in milk they make a pleasant whey. The juice is gratefully acid, and when obtained, and properly evaporated, it yields a crystalline acid salt, denominated oxalic acid, and which is highly estimated wherever vegetable acids are required.

The same is employed for taking iron-moulds out of linen, and is sold under the name of essential salt of lemons.

Worthy of brief notice is the economy of this delicate plant. Although expanding early in the year, and associated with April showers and wandering sunbeams, it does not shrink from the heat of summer. True it is that the botanist cannot find his favourite flower in her usual haunt, by streamlet brink, on wood or heath; but although her delicate white petals are seen only at one season of the year, seed-vessels are produced, and seeds ripen during the greater part of summer; and these, as in many other species, bend downwards during the process of ripening, and when the seed is perfected again become upright. If the seed-vessels are slightly pressed they open at the angles, and their contents are thrown out, not from any elasticity in the capsule, which remains unchanged, but by the expansion of a strong white shiny coating, which enwraps the seed, and which, when acted upon by air or light, suddenly propels it to a considerable distance.

Nor less peerless among her vestal sisters is the Wood-Anemone (*Anemone nemorosa*). Similar in her habitat, being found not unfrequently with the wood-sorrel in woods, or hollow ways, she is one of Nature's weather-glasses; her flowers fold up in a curious manner, and bend towards the earth when showers are abroad; and though occasionally of a purplish red colour, as about Keswick, and in parts of Devonshire, the inner petals are generally of a clear white, while the outer are tinged with purple at the base; and yet the flowers, however beautiful to the eye, are poisonous, and the whole plant yields an acrid, volatile, and corrosive substance, used externally instead of cantharides.

The wood-anemone derives its generic name from a Greek word, signifying the wind, because the slightest breeze scatters its delicate petals to the earth. Garden varieties, and some of the purest white, are derived from Greece; they beautifully enamel her meadows, and grow luxuriantly beside many a classic stream. We may, therefore, infer that a celebrated artist of that country had reference to this flower when he taxed the ingenuity of his intended son-in-law to compose a flower-piece of such only as were perfectly white, half of which were to be painted in their natural colour, the other purple, without deviating from Nature. The young man well knew the effect produced by shadow; he had often noticed the white anemone growing beside the shade of rocks, and observed how dark a hue was cast on its pure white leaves when the deep shadow of the rock began to lengthen on the grass. He might have also seen a group of wild anemones, when the setting sun threw a golden radiance over the fields of Greece, the one part in deep shade, and of a sombre hue; the other gloriously shone upon, and reflecting the empurpled hue of heaven. Be this as it may, he introduced a purple vase into his picture, and represented the light as passing through it on the flower, that drooped over the edge.

Wallflowers (*Cheiranthus fructiculosus*), pre-eminent among such as especially pertain to this showery month, because invariably opening towards the latter end, grow profusely on old walls, and roofs, and rocks, in various parts of England. Its name, *Cheiranthus*, is derived from two Greek words, signifying the hand, and a flower, which probably denotes that its agreeable scent invites the passer-by to stretch forth his hand and gather it; or else that the pods of some species expand like fingers. The small flowers are of pure yellow, and never exhibit the slightest stain; they grow profusely in their favourite haunts: and impart a delicious fragrance. Hence the wallflower has become an emblem of fidelity in misfortune, because attaching itself to desolate places, and enlivening those forlorn and dismantled ruins which otherwise might become repulsive. It conceals the rents of ruin; and where Time has left his stern records the wallflower throws its drapery of bright flowers and light green leaves, as if desiring to obliterate them; it occupies

the ruined breach which war has made, and weaves a garland for the lichen-dotted tomb which even memory has
deserted.

Children delight in this wild flower; its bright hues and
fragrance often lure their young steps to climb some rocky
pathway; and thus beautifully has the northern bard alluded
to a wallflower, when describing the early days of the
"grandame's child"—

> "And well the lonely infant knew
> Recesses where the wallflower grew:
> I deem such nooks the sweetest shade
> The sun in all his round survey'd."

And again—

> "The rude stone fence, with fragrant wallflowers gay,
> To me more pleasure yield
> Than all the pomp imperial domes survey."

The same idea is elegantly expressed by another poet,
who loved the wildest solitudes of Nature, where old ruins
stood in their loneliness, amid ancestral trees, or beside the
dry beds of deserted fish-ponds—

> "Oh, thou lone growing wallflower, to my breast
> And muse art dearest, wildest, sweetest flower!
> To whom alone the privilege is given
> Proudly to root thyself above the rest,
> As genius does, and, from thy rocky tower,
> Lend fragrance to the purest breath of heaven."

Tradition, which preserves the thread of history which
time or war has broken, associates with this fond plant one
of her wildest fantasies. She tells that, in old days, a noble
castle stood alone in its greatness, amid wood and wilds,
and within hearing of the rushing Tweed: that a fair damsel
had long been detained a prisoner within the walls, having
given her heart's affections to the young heir of a hostile
clan; that although the youth was of equal birth, and re-

nowned for feats of arms, blood having been shed between the chiefs on either side, the deadly hatred of those fierce days forbade all thoughts of their union. Time would fail me to speak of the stratagems which the youth devised to get possession of his bride; how he got admission within the walls at one time in the garb of a priest, at another as a wandering troubadour, when he sung at a high festival before his lady-love, till at length, by aid of a serving-woman, it was arranged that the Lady Jane should effect her escape, while the knight awaited her arrival with a noble courser and armed men :—

> " Up then she got upon a wall,
>   Attempted down to slide withal;
>   But the silken twist untied,
>   So she fell, and, bruised, she died.
>   Love, in pity to the deed,
>   And her loving luckless speed,
>   Turn'd her to this plant, we call
>   Now, the Flower of the Wall.''

The Vernal Speedwell (*Veronica verna*) has nought of history nor tradition, neither of poetry nor romance, from which to " point a moral," or weave a tale whereby to enliven the showery April. It grows best on dry and barren soil, and not unfrequently amid driving sands, in which it is nearly buried. The Lesser Celandine (*Ranunculus ficaria*) is seen, on the contrary, in damp meadows, and hedge-banks, and beside rivulets that wind amid high grass and sedges. The generic name is the diminutive of *rana*, a frog; either because some of the species are found in marshy places, or because the divisions of the leaves bear an imaginary resemblance to the foot of that reptile. But wherever found, the rich shining flowers of " the little humble celandine " of the poet Wordsworth, produce a beautiful effect; they are the haunt and home of numerous winged insects, peopled like fairy citadels, and occasionally ornamented with small white parasitic fungi, that contain seeds of the brightest orange.

Beside them grows the brilliant Marsh-Marigold (*Caltha palustris*), from calanthus, a' little basket, which the expanded flower somewhat resembles. The flowers, if gathered before they are fully open, and preserved in salted vinegar, are a good substitute for capers; and their juice, when boiled with a little alum, will stain paper of a beautiful yet evanescent colour. Country people strew the flowers before their doors on May-day, or form them into garlands; and young children seem especially to delight in gathering them from beside the streamlet's rush. What flower more brilliant or attractive, with its large, showy, and slightly concave petals, shining like polished mirrors, and reflecting the sunbeams as they break forth at intervals from among the hurrying clouds, and light up the dewy herbage?

The Scotch name, Gowlan, or Gowan, though indiscriminately applied to several spring-flowers, is generally understood to designate four different kinds of April flowers; namely, the daisy and the dandelion, with the crowfoot and meadow-boat; thus the "gowany glen" signifies, most probably, flowery dales, and is thus mentioned by the poet, Burns—

> "We twa hae run about the braes,
> And pu'd the gowans fine."

Few plants are more ornamental beside the margins of lakes or streamlets in pleasure-grounds. You may see them beautifully reflected on the calm mirror-like surface of the water, while the small white butterfly closes and opens her delicately-tinted wings on their bright disks, in pleasing contrast to the golden hue of that gorgeous flower; and beneath them another flower and another butterfly, though less vivid, seem to arise from out the water with a wavy kind of motion when a light breeze ripples the surface: or large drops from some passing cloud form, in falling, those concentric circles that the passer-by often lingers to admire.

And not less valuable in its medicinal qualities than distinguished for brilliancy of hue, is the beautiful marsh marigold. The gaseous exhalation of plants and flowers are mostly injurious in the night; but those of this aquatic plant have a different tendency. Dr. Withering relates that a large quantity of these flowers having been placed in the bed-room of a girl who was subject to fits, the fits entirely ceased. Hence an infusion of the petals has been successful in various kinds of fits, both with children and adults.

Who does not vividly remember the delight which he felt in childhood when first beholding a Primrose (*Primula vulgaris*) in this favourite month? and still the same delight is renewed from year to year—less vivid, perhaps, yet still recalling many a fond thought and joyous feeling. The primrose, associated with clouds and sunbeams, and the cuckoo's welcome voice, "shines like a star of earth from amid the grass on the brook side, lighting the hand to pluck it." We still feel that it is the primrose of our youth, the primrose after which we often scrambled amid thorns and tangled briers, or which lured our young feet "into the damp grass, and procured for us colds and chiding." There is a sentiment in flowers; and the primrose is one of those which we cannot look upon, nor even hear named, without awakening thoughts of by-gone days.

"Oh! who can speak his joys when Spring's young morn
From wood and pasture open'd on his view;
When tender green buds blush upon the thorn,
And the first primrose dips its leaves in dew!"

MAY.

" THE flowery May,
That from her green lap throws,
The yellow cowslip, and the pale primrose."
                                        MILTON.

COWSLIPS and Primroses especially pertain to May. A few
are seen occasionally at the latter end of April, peeping from
among tufts of moss, on hedge-banks, or along the margin
of clear streams that wend sounding through sheltered
valleys. But now every bank, and meadow, streamlet
edge, and glen, is covered with them.

The Primrose was mentioned in connection with last month:
I shall, however, carry on its history a little further, because
some interesting particulars remain untold.

This small flower has its own brief history associated with
its place of growth, and such insects as find a resting-place
and ready banquet among its hospitable leaves. It affords,
also, an instructive instance of that restriction with regard
to diet which prevails throughout the animal creation.
Cows rarely browse upon the cowslip, horses and swine uni-
formily avoid it; but sheep and goats pluck it not unfrequently in passing—and yet rather as an exception than a
rule. And why? Because if sheep, in pasturing, preferred
flowers to their natural herbage, what would become of the
industrious bee, equally with all such winged creatures that
dwell among the flowers? The humming of the former,
when busy at her work, must cease; and many a beauteous
insect that flits across our path in spring must fail from
want. Seeds, also, would be wanting, and our verdant
meadows would become unprofitable: hence, also, in tracing
further the consequences that must result from any infringe-
ment of that one great law to which the Creator has sub-

jected all herbivorous animals, the cropping of grasses when in flower would necessarily affect those harmless and useful creatures which pasture on them; the flocks would be cut off from the fold, there would be no herds in the stalls: how then could man be clothed or fed? Innumerable manufactures must fail also, and many necessary arts be laid aside.

The cowslip, therefore, and the primrose, remain uncropped even among grass where cattle graze, and the bee and butterfly visit them unmolested! Beautiful are they in their assigned localities, when the winter is over and gone; and he who looks towards the borders of the good green woods fears no longer that their branches will become covered with snow. Then it is that we rejoice in the first nestlings of spring, and love to look upon their meek familiar faces, across which no clouds of sorrow ever pass—on which Time writes no wrinkles.

Single and double varieties are cultivated in gardens; and many, in giving them the preference, affect to disregard the primrose of our banks and hedges—and yet no youthful remembrances are blended with them. It is the sulphur-coloured primrose that best we love; that little flower, "which joyeth," as says old Gerard, "to grow in moist and dankish places, but not altogether covered with water; hence they be found in woods and the borders of dampe meadowes." We do indeed give the name of primrose, as already mentioned, to the double lilac-flower of garden borders; but only from courtesy we like to look upon it, and not with any feeling of peculiar joyfulness, because the pleasure which we derive from flowers chiefly depends on their associations. The common primrose, on the contrary, recalls to mind many a pleasant walk on a summer evening, through meadows, and beside streams, such as the Emperor Charles V. so greatly admired around Florence; when from his palace window, looking on meadows filled with primroses, he said they were too pleasant to look upon, excepting on a holiday.

True it is that the double lilac-primrose of our gardens has no peculiar association wherewith to awaken pleasant thoughts. It is otherwise with the old man who goes forth among the woods of Yorkshire, leaning on his staff, and searching warily for the wild flowers which he gathered on a summer holiday. "There is a strange primrose, found in Yorkshire," wrote Master Gerard in the days of Queen Elizabeth; "it was discovered by the travel and industry of a learned gentleman of Lancashire, called Mr. Thomas Hesketh, a diligent searcher of simples, who hath not only brought to light this amiable and pleasant primrose, but many others also, never before his time remembered or found out. This kind of primrose hath leaves and roots like the wild field-primrose in each respect. It sendeth forth from out its leaves a stalk on which doth grow in winter time one floure, but no more, like unto that in the field; but in summer time it bringeth forth a soft russet hose, wherein are contained many small floures, sometimes foure or five, many times, more, very thick thrust together, which make one entire floure, seeming to be one of the common sorte of double primroses, whereas it is indeed one double floure, made of a number of small single floures, never ceasing to beare floures summer and winter, as before is specified."

But though thus well described by the Simpler, and penned from his words by the indefatigable Gerard, many a truant boy doubtless found the same primrose growing wild among the woods, and brought it home to his little sister, in the days of Queen Elizabeth.

And truly, that great queen, when unvexed by thoughts of the Spanish armada, and her rough suitor Philip of Spain, would have rejoiced to find the double primrose in her morning walk. Feeling strong within her the love of rural sights and sounds, which Cowper has happily denominated an inborn inextinguishable thirst, she often wished herself a milkmaid in the flowery month of May, because, untroubled with cares and fears, such persons sing sweetly all the day, and sleep securely all the night, gathering primroses among the grass, and rising early, when the lark is about to leave her nest.

> In that soft season, when descending showers
> Call forth the greens, and wake the rising flowers;
> When opening buds salute the wakening day,
> And earth relenting feels the genial ray.

Flowers of all forms and hues crowd beside our paths, whether in woods or fields, or on the margin of streams and marshes, making cheerful many a lone swamp with its pollard willow-trees and sedges. The Water-Crowfoot (*Ranunculus aquatilis*), although often regarded as a troublesome weed, produces a beautiful effect when in such profusion as to cover the surface of its aquatic growing-place. The stem is floating and submerged, cylindrical and leafy, and branched according to its depth, and the flowers, upheld on foot-stalks that rise from the same sheath as the leaves, are delicately white, with a yellow spot at the base of each petal. A singular difference is obvious in the leaves of the water-crowfoot; such as grow beneath the surface are hair-like, while such as grow above are lobed and notched, and assume a form consonant to the natural habit of the plant.

Four distinct varieties pertain to this interesting genus. In the large-flowered, none of the leaves are hair-like; in the *circinatus* all the leaves are hair-like, forming a roundish outline; in the *diffusus* they are also hair-like; but the outline is irregular in the *fluviatilis*—the capillary-formed segments are long and parallel, and take the direction of the rapid stream in which they grow. Hence they become exhausted, and rarely produce flowers.

The Oxlip, or Oxlip Primrose (*Primula officinalis*), opening occasionally like its relative in April, yet generally assigned to May, is found most commonly in woods, and hedges, and clayey pastures—but rare, and eagerly sought for by children, wherever it grows.

WATER CROW-FOOT.

The Polyanthus of our gardens is believed to originate equally from the primrose and oxslip; and double and seedless varieties of this family, produced by culture, appear to be almost endless.   The favourite tribe of

> " Auriculas, enrich'd
> With shining meal o'er all their velvet leaves,"

is also derived from the Auricula Primrose (*Primula auricula*), a native of the Swiss mountains.   To the lovers of this tribe we may remark, on our own personal knowledge, that flowers may be rendered of remarkable size and beauty by the application of raw meat to the roots, when the flower-buds are nearly developed.

But the Cowslip (*Primula officinalis*)—that beautiful spring flower, so rare in Devonshire as to grow exclusively about Kent's Hole, near Torquay. Which among the children of Flora may compete with its graceful bell-shaped clusters?

" It is the same; it is the very scent,
   That bland, yet luscious meadow-breathing sweet,
   Which I remember when my childish feet
   With a new life's rejoicing spirit went
   Through the deep grass, with wild flowers richly bent,
   That smiled to high Heaven from their verdant seat.
   But it brings not to thee such joy complete:
   Thou canst not see as I do how we spent,
   In blessedness, in sunshine, and in flowers,
   The beautiful noon; and then, how seated round
   The odorous pile upon the shady ground,
   A boyish group, we laugh'd away the hours,
   Plucking the yellow blooms for future wine,
   While o'er us play'd a mother's smile divine."

Many a fairy legend is connected with this wine-producing flower. The " tiny people "—as legends tell—love to nestle in the drooping bells, with their crimson drops. Hear you not soft music pealing from them, when the moon shines bright, and dew glitters on the grass; sweet voices, too, singing the praises of that sheltering flower, wherein they can await the passing by of showers, when clouds and moonbeams alternate? The poet's eye discerns, it may be, the hurrying of fairy crowds, when pattering rain-drops begin to fall; their gossamer robes—now light, now dark, as leaf-shadows fall upon them, and their anxious tiny faces looking wistfully through the blades of grass for some friendly cowslip. In a moment they are seen clambering up the stalks, rushing each one into the nearest bell; and then a symphony of soft sweet voices is heard proceeding from that same tuft of cowslip; and he who listens, may hear, perchance, a melody of fairyland, now praising the friendly flower—and now somewhat boastful concerning the small kind offices that fairies love to render.

" Now peep'd forth one, right beauteous to behold,
   Whose coat was like a brooklet that the sun
   Had all embroider'd with its crooket gold,

It was so quaintly wrought and overrun
With spangled traceries—most meet for one
That was a warden for the pearly streams;
And as he stept out of the cowslip dun
His jewels sparkled in the pale moon gleams,
And shot into the air their pointed beams.

Qoth he—We bear the gold and silver keys
Of bubbling streams and fountains, that below
Course through the veiny earth—which when they freeze
Into hard chrysolites, we bid to flow,
Creeping with easy course, when, as they go,
We guide their windings to melodious falls,
At whose soft murmurings—so sweet and low—
Poets have tun'd their smoothest madrigals,
To sing to ladies in their banquet halls."

Not less beautiful nor welcome is the Bird's-eye Primrose (*P. farinosa*), a most elegant plant, much smaller than the common primrose, of which the fruit-stalk and calyx appear as if dusted with flour, and the blossoms are bluish red, with yellow eyes. This graceful plant is assigned to marshes and bogs, or mountains in the north; it covers, with its congener, meadows near Kendal, in the richest profusion; growing about Coniston, that favourite among lakes of the gifted Elizabeth Smith, and spreading like a pinky light over meadows that slope towards the water. The mountainous pastures of Westmoreland and Durham, of Cumberland and Yorkshire, are gaily decorated with this somewhat rare plant, as also different marshes near the mouth of the river Dee in Flintshire. Associated, therefore, with many a time-haunted spot, or scenes which poets have loved to describe because of their surpassing beauty, the bird's-eye primrose is a favourite among botanists.

The Scottish Primrose (*P. Scotica*) has long been cultivated in gardens, although its wild growing - places on Holborn Head, near Thurso, in Caithness, as also between Thurso and Dunbeath, have been only lately discovered.

Crowding along the streamlet's brink are innumerable

Daffodils—white one-flowered daffodils, poetic Narcissus (*Narcissus poeticus*), which delight the passer-by with their beauty and fragrance. Greek and Roman poets sung concerning that solitary pure white flower, and its crimson-bordered nectary; they fabled that the self-admiring Narcissus, who loved to gaze for hours on his image in some clear stream, was changed into this flower; that Proserpine

DAFFODIL.

was so attracted by its beauty, as to wander among the meadows during her abode in Sicily, solely occupied in gathering daffodils on the luxuriant plains of Enna.

With equal beauty grows the Pale Daffodil, or Primrose Peerless (*N. biflorus*), in fields and woodsides in the West of England; as also the Common Daffodil (*N. pseudo-narcissus*), which is more generally diffused in woods and meadows, hedge-sides and orchards, and on the margin of streams. I remember their favourite growing-place around the well-head of a clear stream that leaped from out a rocky bank in Gloucestershire. Old trees and saplings grouped round, with bushes of the Wild Dog-Rose (*Rosa arvensis*), pale, and somewhat scentless, yet most welcome, and covering many a hedge with its graceful wreaths; beneath them, yet nearer to the stream, grew innumerable daffodils; and wherever the stream wandered, they followed closely, drooping above the waters, as if loving their reflected images. A thick hedge, that stretched across the meadows, from the upper part of which rushed forth that stream, could not stop them. They found some small opening, and either progressing by means of their roots beneath the ground, or else stooping their slender heads, they still went on, and you might see the brotherhood of yellow flowers on either side the stream- let, far as its windings extended.

That was the place for flowers!—the well-head, and stream, and meadows, seemed to attract flowers of all hues and scents. Periwinkles, the larger and the less (*Vinca minor* and *major*), grew there, extending into large dense patches, with their classic and mournful associations; the one forming in ancient times a bridal belt, whereby to con- fine the long flowing drapery worn by the Roman maiden on her wedding-day, the other used for enwreathing de- ceased infants; and hence its name in modern times " *Tior di morti.*"

Wood Crowfoots, or Goldilocks (*Ranunculus auricomus*) trooped along the margin of a small grove, through which a winding path led onward amid scenes of exquisite beauty; among the grass were tufts of Cuckoo Flowers (*Cardamine pratensis*), that faithful and punctual flower, which heralds the welcome cuckoo; as also common Bugles (*Ajuga reptans*), or Fairy Trumpets, and Sweet Woodruffs (*Asperula odorata*), or Woodderowffe, as spelt by old authors, and of which the repetition of the double letters affords great amusement to children learning to spell. The flower itself is scentless;

but no sooner does it begin to dry, than it exhales a pleasant and lasting fragrance, resembling new hay, yet partaking of the odour of bitter almonds.

Children from a neighbouring hamlet resorted to this wild spot; they fancied that the cuckoo sang there earlier than elsewhere, and they loved to seek out her emblem-flower. You might hear their gleeful voices long before you crossed the stile into the meadows, and many a joyous group used to gather round the well-head—some to hold their hands under the gush of the fresh stream, others to weave small chaplets of flowers and posies of all hues. The high bank often looked purple with the Wild Hyacinth (*Scilla nulens*), or Hare-bell squill, the gentle hare-bell of England, with its pendulous, fine blue, and sweetly-scented flowers. Violets, too, mingled profusely with them; and the greater Stitchwort (*Stellaria polestea*), having large white flowers, and an attendant yellow winged moth, presented a pleasing contrast to the purple Columbine (*Aquilegia vulgaris*), which derives its name from *aquila*, an eagle, and *ligo*, to gather and collect, because the nectaries resemble the claws of that rapacious bird; the softer name of columbine was suggested from the fancied resemblance which they bear still more correctly to the head or neck of the wild dove, which affects their wild habitats.

That pleasing flower often detained the lover of nature to watch the instinctive sagacity of an industrious bee, while bent on obtaining the hoarded sweets. The elongated and incurved nectary of the flower seemed to bid defiance to the entrance of the bee in search of the hidden treasure; but the sagacious insect would not be thus baffled. He might be seen buzzing round the columbine, to ascertain apparently the possibility of effecting an entrance; but finding this impossible, he reaches forth his proboscis, and pierces an opening both in the calyx and blossom, near the depot of nectareous juice, and then extracts the latent sweets without further difficulty.

Such are the most prominent or beautiful among the May flowers. Seek for them in the early morning, when the meadows are sparkling with dew, and the soaring lark warbles his matin lay; there is then an indescribable freshness and loveliness in nature — a lingering, it may be, of that which rested on all created things in the earliest springtide of the year. Very different is the aspect of creation when the sun is high in heaven: you may find the self-same flowers, and walk through the meadows where they grow, or beside the stream, beloved of water-plants, but you will not find the lustre on the leaf, nor yet the beauty on the flower, which he who has risen early everywhere discerns.

> " Oh, who the melodies of morn can tell!
>> The wild brook babbling down the mountain side;
> The lowing herd, the sheepfold's simple bell;
>> The pipe of early shepherd dim descried
>> In the lone valley echoing far and wide;
> The clamorous horn along the cliffs above;
>> The hollow murmur of the ocean-tide;
> The hum of bees, the linnet's lay of love,
> And the full choir that wakes the universal grove."
>
>   BEATTIE.

JUNE.

> " THEIR groves of sweet myrtle let foreign lands reckon,
>> Whose bright beaming summers exalt the perfume;
> Far dearer to me yon lone glen of green breckan,
>> Wi' the burn stealing under the long yellow broom;
> Far dearer to me are yon humble broom bowers,
>> Where the blue-bell and gowan lurk lowly unseen:
> For there lightly tripping among the wild flowers,
>> A listening the linnet, oft wanders my Jean."

THUS sang the poet Burns in praise of that golden-yellow blossomed flower (*Spartium scoparium*), which often bends over headlong torrents, and spreads a gorgeous carpet on

mountain sides, beautiful wherever growing, and yielding
an abundant supply of honey for the bees.

Who may gaze undelighted upon the splendid wreaths of
blossom,

"Yellow and bright as bullion unalloy'd,"

that crown this gorgeous wayside plant, which—thriving
best in sandy soils, or dry fields and thickets—is rarely
molested even by those who, unacquainted with Scottish
pastorals, know nothing of their frequent allusions to the
"Bonnie bonnie Broom!" The boy who in seeking birds'
nests clambers up the rugged bank whereon they grow,
does not willingly tread them down; and when clustering
in the corner of his fields, the farmer often bids his labourer
leave the bright yellow shrubs unharmed. And why is
this, when many a beautiful flower is uprooted? Because
the broom is not only cheerful to look upon, but thrives
among sand, and in stony places of little worth, and its
many valuable qualities are well known in the farmer's
family.

A decoction of green broom tops, with a spoonful of whole
mustard seed, taken every morning and evening, has proved
invaluable in confirmed dropsies. Half a pint is the prescribed quantity; and an infusion of the seeds, drank freely,
have been equally beneficial. The wood is valued for
veneering. As far back as the time of Pliny, fibres obtained
by steeping the branches in water, made enduring fishing-
nets. The tender tops are used as a substitute for hops,
and the seeds, when roasted, resemble coffee. The Italian
peasant constructs, from the long and flexible shoots, bands
wherewith to support his loaded vines : and the northern
matron derives from them an excellent kind of flax, which,
after having bleached, she spins with good success. You
may hear her cheerful voice, singing the songs of her father-
land, in unison with the hum of her spinning-wheel, and
that often in some solitary glen, of which the rocky sides are

covered with golden brooms, beautifully contrasted with dark pine-woods, that sweep over hill and dale, till lost in the far distance. Her "gude mon" covers his cottage roof and rick with thatch made from the young shoots; and in some disforested districts where fuel is scarce, this valuable shrub answers the same purpose.

Carpet brooms are likewise made from the twigs. Children gather them in the spring; they go forth into the rocky valleys, carrying provisions for the day, and return at evening with loaded baskets, from which their parents derive no small advantage. The mention of this useful appropriation recalls to mind those "buy-a-broom" girls, whose picturesque appearance excited no small attention a few years since—but who are now rarely seen. They came principally from Holland, and often obtained sufficient money whereby materially to assist their parents through the winter.

Many a plaintive tale is associated with the broom; many a lament has been written concerning the sad thoughts that are blended with the "long yellow broom," by him who remembers it in connection with his far-off home. What more touching than the following lines, penned by one who recalled to mind the rural occupations of his youth amid the hurry of street-pacing steeds ?—

> "More pleasing far is (Cowden knowes,)
> My peaceful happy home,
> Where I was wont to milk my ewes,
> At e'en among the broom."

History relates that this wild shrub was not less distinguished amid the stormy times of the fourteenth century, even by royalty, than the rival rose herself, for a sprig of the *genista* was adopted as his badge by Gefroi, Duke of Anjou, father of Henry II. He gathered that wild flower, as legends tell, when passing through a rocky pathway; he saw on either side bushes of yellow broom clinging with firm grasp to the huge stones, or upholding the crumbling soil; "and thus," said he, "shall that golden plant ever be my cognizance, rooted firmly amid rocks, and yet upholding that which is ready to fail. I will bear it in my crest, amid battle-fields if need be, at tournaments, and when dispensing justice." Thus saying, the warrior broke off a branch, and fixing it in triumph on his cap, returned to his castle, while as yet the flowers had not drooped. And not only did the duke adopt his country's most beauteous wild flower as a cognizance, he also took the name of Plantagenet, or *Planta genista*, and transmitted the same to his princely descendants, who each bore it from the time of Henry II., called by historians the first Royal sprig of *genista*, till the tyrant Richard, "hunchbacked Richard," last degenerate scion of the plant of Anjou.

> " Time was when thy golden chain of flowers
>   Was link'd the warrior's brow to bind ;
> When, reared in the shelter of royal bowers,
>   Thy wreath with a kingly coronal twined.
>
> The chieftain who bore thee high in his crest,
>   And bequeath'd to his race thy simple name,
> Long ages past has sunk to his rest,
>   And only survives in the rôle of fame.
>
> Though a feeble thing that Nature forms,
>   A frail and perishing flower art thou ;
> Yet thy race has surviv'd a thousand storms
>   That have made the monarch and warrior bow.
>
> The storied urn may be crumbled to dust,
>   And time may the marble bust deface ;
> But thou wilt be faithful and firm to thy trust,
>   The memorial flower of a princely race."

Linnæus, who never saw the Common Furze (*Ulex Europæus*) in Sweden, where the climate is too severe for its spontaneous production, threw himself upon the ground in a transport of enthusiasm, when first beholding its brilliant and widely-entended exuberance. Even strangers who have come from Italy—

"Where the rough rocks with tender myrtles bloom,"

have exhausted the powers of their own musical language in describing their feelings of admiration while looking over some wide moor, covered with furze-bushes in full flower. The odour also, exhaled from myriads of blossoms, when wafted by some gentle gale athwart their path, has called forth the most ardent expressions of delight in great minds, of thankfulness, for being permitted to enjoy the beauty and fragance of such an inimitable flower.

The common furze, though growing on heaths and road-sides in many parts of England, is most luxuriant in Cornwall, where it often attains the height of six or eight feet. It is called Whyn in the east, and Gorse in the north of England; but unlike the broom, which thrives in poor ground, it requires a good soil. Very many are its uses, for the furze is not only a beauteous, but a valuable gift to man, forming a strong fence on the sides of bleak mountains, or close to the sea-side, where the spray thrown by the salt billows destroys almost every other shrub.

These friendly gorses, growing along the wild sea-shore, or ascending nearly to the summit of bleak mountains, suggest many an important thought. Men, in passing, will do well to stop and think of Him who has thus placed them to protect weak and defenceless ones, or to keep off the sharp and damp salt spray from such small plants as spring up beneath their shelter!

And yet, though hardy, and able to resist those cold and pitiless winds that sweep from off the ocean, the gorse has its assigned growing-place. It is rarely found on open moors in the north of England, though lingering in clefts of rocks, or sheltered nooks, at an elevation of two thousand feet above the level of the country. Such bushes as grow on downs in Wales, Devonshire, and Cornwall, frequently assume the appearance of large green dense balls, in consequence of every tender leaf being shorn away by the sheep and rabbits that frequent these places. In Cornwall, where changes wrought by time and war rendered many parts comparatively a desert, the furze is cultivated to great advantage, and is generally cut to make faggots for heating ovens, on account of its burning rapidly, with a great degree of heat. Team-horses may be supported by this plant, if cut young and bruised in a mill to break the thorns, as also riding-horses; and, when mixed with hay, it forms excellent winter food for horned cattle. In proof of which it is related, that, during the Peninsula war, horses and mules belonging to the British army in position before Bayonne, were chiefly supported on this kind of fodder; the practice is likewise general in the south of France, as also the Scilly islands, of which the hills are rendered beautiful by its natural *chevaux de frise* branches, covered with golden blossoms.

According to Evelyn, this valuable shrub was cultivated on poor lands in Devon and Hertfordshire, and yielded a crop of fuel and fodder valuable as that of wheat. Hence laws were passed in the time of William and Mary, which rendered persons amenable to severe punishment who set fire to furze or heath on commons between Candlemas and Midsummer.

In calm and sunny weather, it is pleasant to hear the crackling sound produced by the explosion of the elastic seed-vessels among furze bushes, resembling that of tiny popguns, such as fairies might be supposed to use, if those small people ever disturbed their pleasant revels with warlike deeds.

And as the furze or gorse often spreads like a golden light on moors and hills, so the beautiful family of Heath diffuses a purple hue over the places of their growth.

These plants, though little regarded in happier climates, are rendered subservient to many important purposes on

bleak and barren highlands.   The Scotch peasants construct
walls for their cottages with alternate layers of the Common
Heath, or Ling (*Calluna vulgaris*), and a kind of mortar
made of black earth and straw; they also make their beds
of it, placing the roots downwards, and the tops uppermost,
which are sufficiently soft to sleep upon.

> " Of this old Scotia's hardy mountaineers
>   Their rustic couches form; and there enjoy
>   Sleep, which, beneath his velvet canopy,
>   Luxurious idleness implores in vain."

Withering, when speaking of the heath, well remarks,
that as the ancients were wont to repose on the leaves of
poetic trees, not doubting their powers of inspiration—as
the *Agnus-cactus* was fabled to compose the troubled mind,
the laurel to excite poetic fire, or the bay to suggest martial
visions—why may not the heather couch equally refresh the
weary limbs of the rough mountaineer, and awaken noble
sentiments in minds scarcely less imaginative than those of
the ancient Greeks, and nothing lacking in credulity ?

> " Nor vainly may the heath-flower shed
>   Its moorland fragrance round his head."

A liquor, much in request among the Scots and Picts,
was made in the olden times, by brewing one part malt and
two of the young shoots of heath; and the same still prevails
in the island of Isla.

A fine orange colour is moreover produced from a strong
decoction of the tops, boiled with alum, as also a liquor for
tanning leather; strong and durable ropes are constructed
from the fibres, and the whole plant is available for thatching, and making besoms; it yields good fuel, and is
frequently used for covering drains.

Where heath abounds the honey has a reddish cast, and
strong flavour, unlike that which is produced from wild

thyme; yet innumerable bees pasture upon this luscious plant, on account of its rich nectareous juice. Grouse and heathcocks feed upon the tender shoots; and, in order to preserve for them a continual supply, the seed-vessels are so constructed that a considerable number of seeds are in process of continual development, and when scattered on the earth they rapidly begin to vegetate.

The heath is a beacon-plant; wherever growing, it uniformly denotes that the soil is not calcareous, which circumstance occasions a striking difference between the downs of the more southern counties—where the substratum is chalk—and the wolds of Yorkshire. Heaths, however, though thus restricted, may be seen nestling in the fissures of bleak rocks, and climbing up their rugged sides, from one hundred to three thousand feet above the level of the sea, covered not unfrequently with the bright cobweb-like and elegant pink festoons of the Lesser Dodder (*Cuscuta epithymum*), a parasitic plant which attaches itself especially to the *Erica vagans*, or Cornish double-tipped heath, and flowers in June.

Highlanders, wild wandering over blooming heather, and associating many a fond and tender remembrance with every familiar spot, are acutely sensible to the peculiarly local features of their native country. The heather is to them a memorial plant; and many a brave man, who has fearlessly faced danger in its most appalling form, has been seen to weep like a child when looking upon the simple heather in distant lands. Thus beautifully has a northern poet alluded to the fondness of the Highlander for his native plant :—

> " Flowers of the wild, whose purple glow
>   Adorns the dusky mountain's side ;
>   Not the gay hues of Iris' bow,
>   Nor gardens' gorgeous, varied pride,
>   With all its wealth of sweets could cheer,
>   Like thee, the hardy mountaineer.

> Flower of his dear-loved native land!
>   Alas! when distant, far more dear!
> When he, from cold and foreign strand,
>   Looks homeward through the blinding tear,
> How must his aching heart deplore
> That home, and thee, he sees no more!"

The Fine-leaved Heath (*Erica cinerea*), abounding on dry heaths and in woods, the favourite resort of grouse and ptarmigan, is equally useful with the heath already mentioned. The Cornish or Double-tipped Heath (*E. vagans*), is mentioned by Withering as congenial to the magnesian soil of the serpentine formation.

None, surely, may look upon the Bee-flower without admiration; nor yet upon its frequent companion, the Fly Ophyrs (*O. apifera* and *O. muscifera*); the one closely

THE BEE-FLOWER.

resembling the insect whose name it bears, and found most frequently among short herbage, on commons, or in woods, where the air is pure; the other chiefly affecting meadows and pastures in calcareous soil; both beloved of children, and carefully preserved wherever found.

Beautiful flowers meet the botanist at every step, some belonging to the previous months, and still lingering, as if unwilling to depart; a few preceding the coming month, yet pertaining to her often cloudless skies; and others which the naturalist takes note of as opening most commonly in June. Among these are many of the orchis tribe, concerning which there is little to record, with the exception of the Butterfly and Pyramidal Orchis (*O. bifolia* and *O. pyramidalis*), both of which are interesting to collectors. I have often walked far into the woods in quest of these rare plants, growing in open places, where also the elegant little Eyebright (*Euphrasia officinalis*) opens to the sun. The medicinal properties of this pleasing flower have long fallen into disuse, although frequent mention is made of them in the older writers; and Milton, probably with no small feeling in his days of darkness, thus alludes to them:—

> ———"But to nobler sights,
> Michael from Adam's eyes the film remov'd,
> Which that false fruit that promis'd clearer sight
> Had bred; then purged with *euphrasy* and rue
> The visual nerve, for he had much to see."

JULY.

"THE mead is our study, and Nature our book."

GRASSES, such as Linnæus kneeled beside, and praised the Lord for having made, are now in great perfection. Beautiful are they in their assigned localities; useful too, for they minister to the necessities of men and animals, and such wayfaring creatures as derive from them both food and shelter. But, wherever growing, whether in damp and arid places, or in sultry, or cold regions, they are admirably adapted to meet every possible contingency. Grasses, as Paley has well observed, in spirit, if not in words, are worthy of the most minute inspection. The earth is clothed with them, and its inhabitants principally sustained. Cattle feed upon the leaves, and birds upon the smaller seeds, men also upon the larger; for none require to be told that wheat, and rye, and barley, and oats, belong to this class. In those tribes which are more generally considered as grasses, their extraordinary means and powers of preservation and increase, their hardiness, their almost unconquerable disposition to spread, their faculties of reviviscence, coincide with the intentions of their Creator concerning them. They thrive best even when subjected to a mode of treatment by which other plants are destroyed. The more their leaves are consumed, the more rapidly they increase; the more they are trampled upon by sheep and cattle, the thicker they grow. Many, when apparently dead in hot weather, revive after a sudden shower; the field, or park, which looks dry and brown one day, the next is green and pleasant, and the melancholy bleating of sheep and lowing of cattle is no longer heard; the passer-by may see those harmless creatures cropping the glittering herbage, and seeming to rejoice in the luxuriance that is spread before them.

" Behold the fowls of the air," said our Lord to the multitudes that followed Him; " they sow not, neither do they reap nor gather into barns, yet your heavenly Father feedeth them. Are ye not much better than they ?" Our Lord referred most probably to the ample provision yielded by such grasses as clothe the earth; for although granivorous birds feed occasionally upon fruits that ripen in their season, these are comparatively of short duration; whereas, some kinds of grasses continually reproduce their seeds, and are so constructed as to suit all climates. Such as are assigned to cold and damp countries, or pertain to hills and marshes, carry their flowers in ears, and are frequently surmounted with long awns: they consequently reflect the rays of light, and ripen readily in even the most unfavourable seasons; those, on the contrary, which belong to hot countries, produce their seeds in flowing or drooping plumes, whereby to shelter them from the heat of the sun. Their flexible stems are likewise deserving of remark, as also the admirable manner in which they are strengthened with joints at certain distances. The leaves bear in like manner an obvious reference to the necessities of the parent plant; they are long and slender, and bend readily before the wind without breaking; hence they remain uninjured in the heaviest storms, their weakness becomes their strength, when neither giant trunks nor firmly interlacing roots protect the forest trees.

Thus wonderfully constructed, and endowed with an extra portion of silicious particles, which serve to increase the power of resistance, grasses are found in every part of the known world; among the rocks of Siberia, and in the torrid zone. A spirit of life, independent of all soils and climates, preserves and reproduces them; and while the lesser pyramids of Egypt are falling to decay, grasses which grew around them when the Israelites toiled in the erection of those stupendous masses, continue in their descendants, and many a solitary tuft still waves in the clefts of huge stones that lift their heads amid the sand, reminding the traveller that the arid waste was not always unclothed with verdure. The lofty buildings of Greece and Rome, obelisks and fountains, palaces and temples, the marbles of which were riveted with iron, are known only in their ruins; but innumerable grasses that yield seed for the pasturage of cattle, and the support of small birds, spring beside them in green luxuriance, or else ascend, unbidden, their broken ramparts, and seat themselves among the rents of ruin, with the yellow wall-flower and blue forget-me-not.

By grasses are meant all those plants which have a round, jointed, and hollow stem, surrounded at each joint with a single leaf, long, narrow and pointed, and whose seeds are

contained in chaffy husks.   This is Ray's definition, and we
cannot do better than follow it in selecting some of the most
conspicuous that pertain to the present month.

The Meadow-Foxtail (*Alopecurus pratensis*) and fine Bent-
grass (*Agrostis vulgaris*) present a striking contrast in their
appearance, though equally diffused in meadows and pastures,

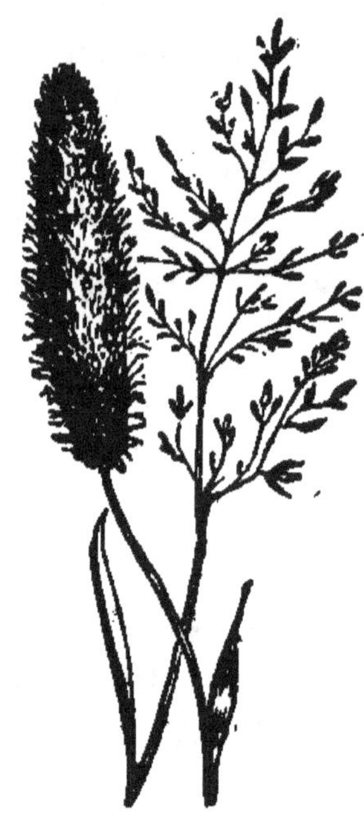

by roadsides and public paths, and, in short, wherever their
services are required.   The first derives its name from two
Greek words, signifying a fox, and a tail, in allusion to the
tufted form of the spike.   It is undoubtedly the best grass
to sow in low meadow ground, or in boggy places that have
been drained, and is often very abundant in rich natural
pastures, where it is eagerly sought by sheep and cattle.
Its brother, the Alpine Foxtail-grass, is so extremely rare
as never to have been discovered excepting on the Scotch
mountains of Loch Na-gore, Clova, and Ben Lawers.

The second belongs to a considerable family, and although
rarely sought by cattle, yields an excellent plat for the
manufacture of hats and bonnets.   One of the most con-

spicuous among its kind is the Marsh Bent-grass (*A. alba*), concerning which botanists relate that, although occasionally denounced as couch-grass, and difficult to eradicate, on account of its wiry and brittle roots, it produces hay preferred by cattle to all others, and is doubtless the real *Fiorin*, or Butter-grass of the Irish; yielding an enormous produce, and equally serviceable for winter green food, by which succulent provender milch cows may be supported from December until late in April. And as its culture is required for pasturage, the slightest soil suffices to nourish its extensively-creeping stem; it is, moreover, in a great degree indifferent to the extremes of dryness, or of moisture, and is found on mountain sides, at different elevations, even on the verge of perpetual winter, being totally insensible to the severity of cold: and in such sterile places, beneath a burning sun, as all other plants instinctively avoid. The fiorin also abounds equally on sandy moors and wet morasses; on thin dry soil as well as moist—extending up the bleakest mountains, and over the shelterless tracts of Dartmoor and Exmoor—or those of Scotland, Ireland, and North Wales. Nor is this all! It seems as if the butter-grass lingered till the beauty or luxuriance of its relatives had passed by, for it remains inactive till other grasses have attained perfection, and become exhausted: then it is that this friendly plant unfolds its productive powers, and the latest mouthful of green herbage, as also occasionally the earliest, is afforded by the fiorin. Such are the united testimonies of Dr. Richardson and Mr. Sinclair, in favour of the marsh bent-grass and its numerous relatives. Varieties, however, pro·duced by accidental circumstances, and possessing a tenacity of growth that does not yield even to ploughing or pulverizing, has caused this generally-diffused grass to be disliked by many agriculturists.

The Silky Bent-grass (*A. spica venti*) may be easily distinguished from other grasses, in sandy fields, or among corn, by its silky panicle, about eight or twelve inches long,

leaning on one side, and of a somewhat purple hue. After
the spring-sown corn has vegetated, and until the ripening
of harvest-fields, flocks of pigeons diligently occupy themselves in picking out the seeds and panicles of the silky
bent-grass with the utmost perseverance. The seeds are,
however, somewhat difficult to obtain, on account of the
long awns; and hence the old couplet:—

> "The pigeon never knoweth woe,
> Until a benting she doth go."

But the chief granary of small birds is the Bird-knot Grass,
or Red Robin (*Polygonum avicularæ*), which abounds on
roadsides, and may be even seen in streets, where a sparrow,
or perchance honest robin, snatches a billful of its tempting seeds, and then darts swiftly away. The plant is not
easily destroyed, though trampled upon by men and animals;
and is so abundant in fields, that the scattering of its innumerable seeds often gives a reddish hue to the ground, after
the gathering in of harvest.

Among such grasses as have been naturalized, the Canary
Grass (*Phalaris canariensis*) is one of the most conspicuous;
and widely-extended crops pleasingly diversify the Isle of
Thanet during the present and coming months.

Meadows continually present an inexhaustible variety of
vegetable forms, small though they be, and such as many
pass unheeding with their sketch-books in their hands, when
seeking for the magnificent or graceful among forest trees.
Grasses are, indeed, comparatively minute, and yet the
painter or the poet may find among them the embodying of
ideal beauty, and that minuteness of embellishment which
is incompatible with grander outlines. Take, for example,
the *Cynodon dactylon*, or Creeping Dog's-tooth grass, ascertained by Sir William Jones to be the Durva, or Dub-grass
of the Hindoos, concerning which he remarks, "that the
flowers in their perfect state afford the loveliest object in
creation, and that, when examined with a microscope, they

resemble emeralds and rubies trembling in the slightest breath of air. Nor is the species less esteemed for its valuable qualities; it forms the sweetest and most nutritious pasturage for cattle; and its usefulness and beauty induced the Hindoos, even in the earliest ages, to believe that it was the dwelling-place of a benevolent and presiding nymph, who loved to listen to the cropping of dewy herbage by flocks and herds in meadows, and beside clear streams. Poets feigned that, looking forth from her diverging spike, adorned with purple flowers, and ranged in two close alternate rows, wherever she presided, there blights and mildews were unknown, and that the air came loaded with fragrance as if from bowers of balm, although neither roses, citrons, richly-scented magnolias, nor orange trees, grew contiguous." Even the Veda celebrates this inimitable grass in the following sentence of the A't'harvana:—" May the Durva, which arose from the waters of life, and which hath a hundred roots and a hundred stems, prolong my existence on earth for a hundred years!"

The Tall Oat-grass (*Avena elatior*) is equally beautiful as the durva, and does not require the assistance of a microscope to develop its perfections. Who has not frequently admired this stately grass in meadows, though, perhaps, unacquainted with its name, which rises to the height of six feet, with leaves of considerable length, and more than an inch wide, and adorned with a panicle of gently-drooping flowers often a foot in length, so finely polished, that notwithstanding their emerald hue, they might be mistaken for silver oats? Yet their colour, though assuming occasionally a green tint, is not really green, neither is it white, nor gold colour, nor purple, but a union of all these; at one moment it resembles gold, at another silver, at another amethyst, according as a passing breeze causes it to quiver in the sunbeams. Truly the grass is exceedingly variable as regards its tints, but this only enhances its loveliness; and when fully ripe, none of its sisters can be compared with the tall oat-grass in its full pride of beauty. The light purple pyramid by which it is distinguished is seen in every field and meadow, in pastures and lanes, and in damp and swampy places, as if in even the most uninviting solitudes the mind might have somewhat to dwell upon suggestive of pleasant thoughts.

The Northern Holy-grass (*Hierochloe borealis*), thus named by Gmelin from two Greek words implying sacred, and a grass—because in Prussia the plant is strewed before the doors of churches on festival days—yields a delightful fragrance, resembling that of the sweet-scented Vernal-grass, (*Anthoxatum odoratum*), which principally occasions the smell of new-mown hay. This kind of grass, though rare in England, and first discovered in the narrow mountain valley of Kella, in Angus-shire, grows exuberantly in Sweden, and is sold for the purpose of being suspended over beds, in order to promote sleep.

The geography of plants, though most conspicuous among forest trees, from the imperishable firs of Norway to the palms and cocoa that belong to exotic regions, is yet strongly marked in our meadows and beside the village pathways. The Crested Dogtail grass (*Cynosurus cristatus*) is plentiful in dry pastures, and yields, in common with several kinds of perennial grasses, a material for the manufacture of Leghorn hats and bonnets, superior to Italian straw. The downy Feather-grass (*Stipa pennata*) grows on mountainous rocks, and is readily distinguished from its brethren by long awns, adorned with fine, white, soft, pellucid and diverging hairs, which so much resemble the plumes of a Bird of Paradise as to be substituted by ladies for that elegant ornament. The awns remain permanently attached till the seeds become fully ripe, when, still retaining their graceful appendage, and barbed with sharp bristles, they are borne hither and thither by the breezes of autumn, and scattered over heath and rock, where they find a resting-place, and spring up with renewed beauty to reward the researches of the botanist, who often ascends with difficulty to their rugged habitats. Such was, but unhappily is not, the home of this favourite among British grasses. My ancestor, Thomas Lawson, when searching for plants in company with Dr. Richardson, found a tuft on the limestone rocks adjoining the valley of Long-leasdale, about six miles from Kendal. Since then, it has only been once discovered in the same spot, and has now disappeared from among the catalogue of British plants. Still, however, the species is carefully cultivated by floral gardeners, and may be seen in company with exotic strangers, as if looking from the windows of richly-decorated show-rooms on the " ever moving myriads" that pass along the streets of London. It seems to me strangely out of place, and my thoughts turn involuntarily to the mountain side, with its fresh pure air, and the small green valley, where grew the tuft of feather-grass when discovered by my gifted ancestor.

The Purple Melic-grass (*Melica cærulea*), on the contrary, grows best where even the hardy lichen is injured or de-stroyed. It is found in boggy, sterile meadows, and grows abundantly in the vicinity of the copper-works at Parys mountain, in Anglesey, where the air is rendered impure and vegetable life speedily becomes extinct. Were it possible to ascertain facts connected with the natural history of this small plant, we should find, most probably, that by the emission of pure oxygen, an atmosphere is formed around its long and flexible leaves, and large purple panicles, by which some tiny insect is enabled to exist in the midst of an otherwise unwholesome region; but why the plant and insect are thus stationed is a problem which none may solve.

The Soft Brome-grass (*Bromus mollis*), though disliked by farmers, must not yet be wanting in his fields. It grows there equally unbidden and unwelcome, and though its use has not been discovered, the awn presents a familiar instance of the wonderful mechanism by which a simple seed is enabled to make its way into the ground when so thickly covered with herbage that the heart of man would be unavailing to effect such a purpose. A continual motion is occasioned by the awns being very susceptible to atmospheric changes, curling up in dry weather, and relaxing with moisture, and thus empowering the seed to push through every intervening obstacle, and at length to bury itself in the soil. Seeds of the bearded Wild Oat-grass (*Avena fatua*) make a lodgment in like manner; and Linnæus tells us, that if the bearded oat is housed with other grain, the plumes speedily become empty. The awns are, therefore, used for hygrometers; and children are delighted with their animated movements, when, after being thrown into water, and then placed on a dry table, they leap and twist about in a most extraordinary manner. The species are found chiefly on clays and stiff gravels.

Marshy places and stream sides are often beautified during the present month with the tall stems and mace-like brown spikes of the Great Cat's-tail, *Typha latifolia* of the ancient Greeks, thus named from a bog or marsh, its natural growing place. The down of the amentum is used to stuff cushions and mattrasses; and in common with its relatives, the Lesser and Dwarf Cat's-tail (*T. angustifolia* and *T. minor*), few, if any, among aquatic vegetables are equally ornamental. The larger species, especially, are often planted on the margin of pools, where they afford an excellent shelter for wild-fowl, and where their spikes present conspicuous and pleasing objects, especially when contrasted with the drooping purple brown and graceful panicles of the common reed (*Arundo pragmites.*)

"The Common Reed!" some one may perhaps exclaim, "growing everywhere, by lakes and rivers, and even roadside ditches! can this homely plant have aught of history or utility?" "Much of both," the botanist replies. Swamps, and low lands occasionally overflowed with water, may be rendered productive if first planted with reeds; and the young shoots cut off close to the ground make excellent pickles. Surely it is also no small praise, that the sedge warbler, a very pretty bird, that frequents osier and willow beds, and warbles her simple yet melodious song from among their branches, prefers suspending her elegantly-formed nest between the stems of two near reeds, at a short distance above the ground. In Sweden the panicles as used for dyeing woollen cloth green, and the reeds are far more durable than straw for thatching. So valuable are they, that in our own fen-counties, when broken down by numerous flights of starlings that annually resort to them, the injury is attended with considerable loss. Garden-screens, whereby to keep off cold winds in spring from tender plants, are made with reeds; and they are laid across the frame of woodwork as the foundation of plaster floors. Artists well know their value, and use them for pens when freedom is required in sketching or etching; and till the introduction of goose-quills for writing, in the seventh century, they were in general request by scribes who often spent their lives in transcribing and illuminating some valuable work. Archers also preferred them for shafts when bows and arrows were in use, hewing with strong hatchets bows from aged yew-trees, and searching along the margin of some neighbouring swamp for the pliant reed. And thus has the plant of which we speak been often quoted as emblematic of a flexible disposition, because bending with the current, or forming the swiftly-flying arrow, in contrast with the tough yew-bow.

The *Arundo arenaria*)Sea-mat Weed, or Bent) pertains to the same family, and is everywhere an object of peculiar interest. Assigned by its Creator to grow on the sea-coast, it offers an effectual barrier to those drifts of sand which often lay waste the fields, and have even destroyed considerable villages. Wherever the sea-mat takes root, a sand-hill presently accumulates, and in proportion as this increases, the friendly plant lifts its head above the surface; hence, most probably, the origin of those round-topped hills, called

links, that extend along many of our northern coasts. The
sea-mat grows profusely on the sands near Liverpool, where
it was planted some years since, in order to bind them
together; as also on the Cornish coast. Queen Elizabeth
prohibited its extirpation, and a recent law protects this
plant throughout the places of its growth.

Few, if any, in the vegetable world, are more wonderfully
constructed, with an obvious reference to the purpose for
which they are designed. The ridged stems are two or
three feet high, the leaves are pointed and thorn-like, and
the roots penetrating. No other mode of structure would
answer the same intent; the penetrating roots fix the plant
firmly; the ridged stems readily resist sand-drifts, however
sudden, and the pointed thorn-like leaves allow the sand to
fall between them as through a sieve, from which the wind
may not again chase it. Now, if the leaves were broad, like
those of the giant coltsfoot, which pertains to March, or if
the stems grew higher, and were light and yielding like the
common rush, the same purpose could not be effected. But
here everything harmonises. The sand is adapted to the
plant, the plant to the sand; the leaves, too, are defended
with a firm hard cuticle, which effectually prevents the fine
particles of salt that fly from off the waves from penetrating
into the pores. Without this admirable provision, the
arundo would soon perish; and if we could examine the
structure of the leaf, we should, doubtless, discover that the
outer surface is endued with a filtering power, by means of
which sufficient moisture is derived from the atmosphere for
its well-being.

Beside the *arundo* often grows another plant, which lends
its aid to prevent the spreading of loose sand on the sea
shore. This is the upright Sea-Lyme grass (*Elymus arena-
rius*), which possesses the singular property of remaining
unmoved in its baseless habitat, and which is common on
most of our sea-coasts. The stems are three or four feet
high, reed-like, and hollow, and the leaves are rolled inward,

and sharp pointed; the sand, therefore, which the sea-mat stops in its hurrying course, and collects around it, the lyme-grass secures, and thus they act in concert, conferring incalculable benefits, and promoting the well-being of mankind.

Such flowers as beautify our fields and meadows in July, open equally in August; and while the mowers have yet spared many a field of waving grass, I have sought to associate with the loveliest, or most useful, some natural or historic facts of considerable interest.

But as botanists in general are now intent on preserving specimens of beautiful or rare plants, I shall transcribe for them a method which I have often tried with the happiest success. It is as follows:—Place the plant, when fresh, between several sheets of blotting-paper, and iron it with a *large* smooth heater, pretty strongly warmed, till all the moisture is dissipated. The flowers may be afterwards fixed down with gum to the paper, and then ironed again, by which means they become almost incorporated with the paper. In general I have preferred tacking the plant with fine cotton to the place where it is destined to remain. Some plants require a more moderate heat than others; experience must determine this, and herein consists the nicety of the experiment.

In compound flowers, as the *Centaurea*, some little art is required in cutting away the under-part, by which means their profiles will be distinctly exhibited—but then they must be pasted down; or else, before ironing, place folded pieces of blotting-paper all round the flower, to make it on a level with the surface.

AUGUST.

> " NOT a flower
> But shows some touch in freckle, streak, or stain,
> Of his unrivall'd pencil.   He inspires
> Their balmy odours, and imparts their hues,
> And fills their cups with nectar."

CONSPICUOUS among such plants as pertain to the present and past month, lingering also among the matron beauties of August, is the *Linnæa borealis*, or Two-flowered Linnæa, an humble Lapland flower, yet immortalzied by its association with that great philosopher, and thus named in allusion to his unobtrusive habits.

This small wild flower was first selected by Gronovius, with the concurrence of Linnæus, as his memorial plant; an adoption rendered peculiarly appropriate by exquisite beauty, sweet odour, and unyielding repugnance to exchange the silent glen and deep pine-wood for the greenhouse or garden border.   "Cultivation," as a Swedish traveller has elegantly remarked, "to her is death; the spirit of the little beauty is broken if you attempt to remove her from the mossy turf and shady haunts in which she blooms, and vain is the most soothing attentions of the gardener."   A friend, in describing this little floweret, unconsciously expressed himself in his broken English in terms full of genuine poetry, when walking by the shores of the lake near Charlottendal, on a lovely evening, and conversing of Linnæus. " I gathered a small flower," said the narrator, "and asked if it was the *Linnæa borealis*, not having then seen it."   He answered, " Nay, she lives not here! but in the middle of our largest woods, where nought is heard but the cuckoo and the rustle of the trees; she spreads her little arms close to the moss, and seems to resist very gently if you tear her from it.   She has a complexion like a milkmaid; and ah!

she is very, very sweet and agreeable." The little flower is truly all this, and as a floral link and memento of her great namesake, possesses attractions which many costly and magnificent creations cannot boast. The author of *Rambles in Sweden and Gottland* tells us further, that the walks which he afterwards took in search of the two-flowered Linnæa were equally numerous and pleasing, but that at length he could not find it in his heart to pluck the little woodland beauty, which seemed to sigh when his hand approached her, as if telling him that she could not live elsewhere. Once, however, he forgot his better feelings; having met with a large party of botanical pilgrims going in search of the Linnæa borealis, he joined them, and went into the romantic pine-woods of Tull-garn, a palace belonging to the king of Sweden, with its long avenue of ash and oak, and rock and lake, shaded with magnificent pines, beneath which grew profusely the sweet little flowers which they sought. Great pains were taken to remove both earth and moss, that the wood-loving plants might be tempted to forget their native haunts—that still, striking their tiny roots in native soil, and seeing around them abundance of friendly mosses, they might become reconciled to a different mode of life. Vain were all attempts. Such of the Linnæa as the narrator obtained drooped and died before he reached home, and caused him to regret more than ever having stolen them from their favourite growing-place.

The two-flowered Linnæa, though most luxuriant in her native country, has also been discovered in England, by Miss Emma Trevelyan, in an old fir-plantation at Catherside, Northumberland. The deep pine-woods of Inglismaldie and Crabstone, in Scotland, likewise shelter this memorial plant, of which the blossom, white outside, pink-coloured within, emits a fragrant odour like the *Spiræa*, which often betrays her solitary home.

Plants and flowers, in all ages, have been the symbols of countries and of kingdoms, or of men who have adorned and improved humanity. It was therefore due to Linnæus, that the loveliest and most fragrant, though least known among Swedish flowers (because it grows in the depths of her vast forests), should thus become his characteristic badge, and bear his name.

Associated also with the magnificent ruins of Wisby, where eighteen time-struck churches or cathedrals and upwards of forty embattled towers attest its ancient splendour, the Linnæa grows nowhere more profusely than in the wild contiguous forests of Gottland. In passing through them the Swedish traveller was everywhere attracted by her beauty. " The woods," he said, " were absolutely perfumed by the Linnæa, which threw up her tiny bells in true woodland pride; thousands of melodious birds made the loneliest places ring with their joyous chorus, while the melancholy tinkle of straying herds was wafted by the wind, as they browsed in the cool sequestered dells, and completed the accompaniments of a forest scene that teemed with life and beauty."

Such are the native haunts of the flower of Linnæus. And not less beautiful and replete with historic interest are the frequent growing-places of the *Carduus heterophyllus*, or Melancholy Thistle, which thrives best in mountainous pastures, and is also abundant in the Roslin and Auchindenny woods. The thistle has long been regarded as the symbol of Scotland, but few are perhaps acquainted with the circumstance that gave rise to its appropriation. Time was when a company of bearded men, with high-crowned hats and doublets, met in solemn consultation within the walls of the old Council-house at Edinburgh, and the subject of their deliberation was the desirableness of placing the thistle on their banner instead of the figure of St. Giles, which had borne many an Highland storm for ages past, and had floated proudly over many a battle-field. This memorable council was convened about the middle of the fifteenth century, and hence the melancholy thistle shortly afterwards became conspicuous on every banner throughout Scotland. It had previously been deemed the badge of the House of Stuart, whose princes were wont to wear the *Cluas-an-pheidh*, for such is it called in Gaelic; and yet as the token-flower of resistance, it is far less illustrative of the national motto, "*Nemo me impune lacessit*," than several of its congeners; the woolly-headed thistle especially, or Friar's Crown (*Carduus eriophorus*), and the Spear-Thistle (*C. lanceolatus*), the first, growing not unfrequently to the height of five feet, with a large purple or white blossom, and lobed leaves that point alternately either downward or horizontally; the second, an emblem of beneficence, for if a heap of clay be thrown up, nothing would grow upon it for many years, were it not that the seeds of this friendly plant, wafted thither by the wind, speedily vegetate, and throwing wide their deep green leaves, which are cottony underneath and hairy above, form a cover for lesser plants. Beautiful flowers soon mantle the otherwise unsightly heap of clay; the small blue forget-me-not, the mouse-ear hawkweed (one of the loveliest of " Flora's-watches," with her numerous relatives of wood and wall); the eye-bright and wild bugle grow there profusely, as also many a meek-eyed sister, who peeps from beneath the leaves of the guardian thistle.

One of the most stately, and yet most lovely of British plants is the tall Purple Foxglove (*Digitalis purpurea*), which affects hedge-banks and the sides of hills, in dry, gravelly, and sandy soils, but is rarely met with in flat, or even mountainous parts. It happens, therefore, that the foxglove is very common in the midland and western, though extremely rare in the eastern counties; that it abounds in the county of Durham, but becomes scarce northward of the Tyne, with the exception of an open space in the vicinity of Rothbury, and a rocky dingle near Roathley.

The geographical limits of the foxglove are consequently well defined, because the seeds, when sown in flat and watery grounds, germinate, and produce flowers at their appointed season; but the roots, which are otherwise biennial, uniformly decay in winter. But even when assigned to gravelly or sandy soils, this graceful plant has its favourite haunts. The heights of Haldon, above Teignmouth, on the roadside leading to Dawlish, is one of these; many acres are thickly and gorgeously covered with its rich purple, rod-like, and terminal spikes; and among the ruins of Tintern Abbey specimens have been gathered which measured in height seven feet nine inches, the length of the spike four feet ten inches, and the number of flowers thereon were seven hundred and eleven! Nor are its purple, elegantly-mottled, and inversely conical bells undeserving the attention of entomologists; a variety of tiny beings, attracted by the shelter or rich repast which the blossoms yield, continually resort to them, and—

> ——"Bees that soar for bloom,
> High as the highest peak of Furness Fells,
> Will murmur by the hour in foxglove bells."
>
> WORDSWORTH.

This beauteous plant was not unknown to the ancients on account of its medicinal qualities; and its celebrity as a vulnerary became, in Italy, during the middle ages, a common proverb. Those who are best acquainted with the history of medicine can tell how often the virtues of different plants have been discovered, lauded, universally applied, and then consigned to oblivion: such, however, has not been the fate of the plant concerning which we speak; the virtues ascribed to it by the first discoverer, in past ages, was acknowledged by the late Dr. Withering. This eminent physician and botanist was engaged in studying, during at least ten years, the properties of foxglove, and clearly substantiated its claim as yielding a most important remedy in pulmonary cases, in controlling the action of the heart, and also in relieving various kinds of dropsy and nervous excitement.

> " The foxglove leaves, with caution given,
>   Another proof of favouring Heaven
>   Will happily display :
>   The rapid pulse it can abate,
>   The hectic flush can moderate,
>   And, blest by Him whose will is fate,
>   May give a lengthen'd day."

The generic name, *digitalis*, is derived from *digitus*, a finger ; its flower, resembling the finger of a glove, is called occasionally the finger-flower, and is so named by Fuchsius, after its German designation.

What plant more beautiful than the Rose-Bay Willow-herb (*Epilobium angustifolium*), growing profusely in woods and meadows, and planting itself in Furness Fells, above Langton Ford, and other inaccessible rocks among the Cheviots ; as also on the Pentland hills, where its rose-coloured, or delicately white blossoms, may be seen waving in the breeze of August, looking cheerful in its high growing-place, and bidding those who pass beneath to look up and consider how one of the most delicately-formed of British plants is sustained in a meagre soil, and remains unbroken, though winds and tempests are abroad ? Pleading, as from an academic chair, concerning much that is profitable and worthy of remembrance, and urging mournful or desponding ones to cast away their care, and to believe that as the brown, storm-beaten rock sustains some flower that, perchance, may not thrive in sheltered places, so every condition in human life has its appropriate blessing.

Epilobium is derived from two Greek words, expressive of a beautiful flower growing upon a pod ; the red blossoms being singularly placed in a lateral position.

The top shoots of its relative, the Large-flowered Willow-herb (*E. hirsutum*), have a delicate acidulous fragrance, resembling scalded codlings, but so transitory as scarcely to be perceptible after being gathered. This gaudy species produces a beautiful effect in moist hedges, and on the banks of streams and ponds, especially when contrasted with the angular and prickly stem of the *Dipsacus fullonum*, or Fuller's Teasel, which is often seen in hedges and rude uncultivated spots.

The name *dipsacus*, derived from a Greek word signifying thirsty, was given in allusion to the peculiar construction of the leaves, that form cavities capable of containing water. Botanists recognize three species of this invaluable genus— the wild (*D. sylvestris*); the shepherd's rod, or small teasel (*D. pilosus*); and the one above-mentioned. The Wild Teasel affords a fine example of what is called the connate leaf, the reservoirs formed by the united leaves frequently retain, in rainy weather, half a pint or more of water, which sustains the parent plant during long drought. In hot countries many a feverish and weary traveller would thankfully exchange all he possesses for a draught from some vegetable fountain; but in this, our pleasant land of wells and running streams, the water thus retained by the wild teasel is only beneficial to the plant itself, or, perchance, to some wayfaring birds in places where rills are scarce.

This plant grows most frequently in uncultivated places, though never discovered north of Derbyshire and Nottinghamshire, and on banks where the moisture which it requires is often dried up. Hence the singular construction of the leaves, which retain every drop that falls from a passing shower, is essential to its well-being.

The Small Teasel affects similar places. It is pleasingly associated with the natural historian of Selborne, who speaks of it as being frequent in one of his favourite walks; with the Lady-well also, a small clear stream, in a solitary lane leading from Norton to the old Roman Watling Street, Northamptonshire.

The vast woollen-clothing fabric materially depends on the fuller's teasel, which is found in hedges and wild sterile spots, and is cultivated to a large extent in the stiff clay lands of Gloucestershire and Somersetshire, of Wiltshire and

Essex. This plant, with the Dutch rush, or shave-grass, of which the stems have long been imported from Holland to polish cabinet-work, ivory, plaster-casts, and even brass, afford the only known instances of natural productions being applied to mechanical purposes.

The teasel is alone available to raise the nap from woollen cloths, and for this purpose the heads are fixed round the circumference of a large broad wheel, which is made to turn in contact with the cloth; if a knot, or roughness, or projection, catch the hooks, they break immediately, without injury; but any mechanical invention, instead of yielding, tears them out, and materially injures the surface.

A pleasing little flower, called the Forget-me-not (*Myosotis palustris*), fringes many a springy bank during this hot month. Pre-eminent among such of its companions in wood or field as awaken thoughts of sadness or affection,

> "Or tell
> What words can never speak so well,"

the Forget-me-not recalls to mind an event connected with the days of chivalry, when Lord Scales, brother to the Queen of Edward IV., tilted against a French knight of Burgundy, and when the ladies of the court playfully presented a collar of gold, enamelled with these brilliant little flowers, to the English knight, for an emprise of arms either on horseback or foot.

SEPTEMBER.

> " Oh, who that has an eye to see,
> A heart to feel, a tongue to bless,
> Can ever undelighted be,
> With Nature's magic loveliness!"

MANY corn-fields are yet unreaped, and there is something indescribably pleasing in their aspect at the commencement of the autumnal season. Flowers of various descriptions are everywhere conspicuous; some—like the *Scandix pecten*,

or common Shepherd's Needle, with its small white petals,
and long graceful tubes; or the Heart's-ease (*Viola tricolor*),
a low-growing yellowish white species, which hide beneath
the arching grain—must be carefully sought for in their
lowly birth-places; others lift up their heads, and beautifully
diversify the rich brown rustling surface of the field. Such
is the *Convolvulus arvensis*, or small Bindweed, which
twines around the stalks, like the thyrsus of living green;
her lot is humble, and she has not to bear the sternness of
wintry storms, therefore she is not defended with a strong
cuticle; but her leaves are slight and fragile, and her petals
sometimes of a yellow hue, but more frequently pink, varied
with white plaits; and he who passes by often lingers to
observe her symmetry and beauty. Lovely indeed she is,
as I once observed elsewhere; and the botanist may recount
concerning her, that she has an assigned duty which no
other flower could fulfil. One day comprises her short life;
but in that one day no work which she has to do is left
undone, and wonderfully is she constructed for the doing of
that work. Her trumpet-shaped corollas, tiny though they
be when compared with the large dazzling white flowers of
her relative, the favourite of St. Pierre, are designed to
reflect the rays of the sun, and, like highly-polished mirrors
directed to one focus, convey as much heat as possible to
the interior. Those who are interested in the admirable
arrangement of the vegetable world, may discern by this
simple token that the small convolvulus is designed to grow
in open and wind-haunted places, or beneath the shade of
taller vegetable forms. She is endowed also with an instinctive motion, by which she is enabled to rise from her
humble or thickly-tangled place of growth, by twining
around the stems of neighbouring plants; and in thus effecting her exit, her spiral stems turn uniformly from west
to south-west; others, on the contrary, perform the same
movement from east to west. Such natural indications
prove unerring guides to travellers when journeying through
pathless solitudes.

A matin flower is this same wild convolvulus—displaying
her small trumpet when the sun rises, and putting it aside
as no longer needful when evening draws in: hinting—it
may be in unison with many a wayside weed that open and
close their petals at stated seasons, with the matin and even-
songs of grateful birds—concerning duties which some unhappily forget, and others but carelessly fulfil. A hospitable flower, too, is she, and winged insects are her guests:
a loving plant, methinks, for I have seen her in company
with her meek sisters, mantling the graves of lowly ones—
yet not in a village churchyard, where the pure air of
heaven comes and goes, and bright sunbeams gladden the
lone spot, but in a burying-ground contiguous to a poor-
house, and that in the neighbourhood of London, beside a
dusty public road. Beautiful were they in that strange and
uninviting place; many stayed their steps to look upon
them, and thought, perchance, of far-off village commons
and bordering cornfields, where they had first gathered the
small convolvulus.

The purplish red Corn-Cockle (*Agrostemma githago*), which
derives a generic name from two Greek words signifying a
field and coronet, is likewise trumpet-shaped, and rises to
the height of two or three feet; nor less conspicuous is the
Red Campion, or Campion Cuckoo-flower (*Lychnis dioica*), signifying a lamp, in allusion to the flame-coloured and flicker-
ing petals; or, as some conjecture, from a fanciful resemblance of the semi-transparent calyx to a lantern. Different
species of the lychnis produce double flowers, either red or
white, and are therefore often sought for by the florist.
But wherever growing, whether among corn or pastures, or
fallow fields, or springing from the fissures of rocks, as those
of Craig Breiddin, in Montgomeryshire, or beside streams of
water, they are objects of no ordinary interest, from the
brightness or extreme delicacy of their deeply-cloven petals.

The *Scabiosa arvensis*, or Field Scabious, is one of my
favourite plants; her delicate blue, or bluish lilac, or even

white globular head, formed of numerous florets, with white
taper bristles appended to each, look well among the waving
ears of corn.　Unlike her sable-tinted sister, the mourning
widow, or musk-button, which St. Pierre describes in his
story of "Paul and Virginia," the species to which I refer
presents a cheerful aspect, and no other plant is more frequently resorted to by gay-coated insects and bright butterflies, that find a resting-place on the tufted florets, and
close and open their wings in the warm sunbeams.　The
Cyanus, corn-flower, hurt-sickle, or blue-bonnet (*Centaurea
cyanus*), often grows beside the scabious; they delight in
the same locality, but the cyanus is best known and most
beloved of poets :—

> " There is a flower, a purple flower,
> 　Sown by the wind, nursed by the shower,
> 　O'er which Love breathed a powerful spell,
> 　The truth of whispering hope to tell.
> 　Now, gentle flower, I pray thee tell,
> 　If my lover loves me, and loves me well :
> 　So may the fall of the morning dew
> 　Keep the sun from fading thy tender blue."

This beauteous flower was named cyanus, after a youthful
devotee of Flora, who made garlands for public festivities
with different kinds of wild flowers, and who often lingered
from morning till evening among the corn, weaving such as
she collected, and singing the sweetest strains of her father-
land.

What an exquisite coronet of sky-blue florets is conspicuous in the Cyanus ! every floret is a fairy vase, that holds
forth a rich nectareous juice to thirsty insects.　And when
each vase, having fulfilled its appointed purpose, is laid
aside, beautiful green cradles become developed, as if by
enchantment, containing little winged children which the
zephyrs delight to rock !　These winged children are often
peculiarly beautiful : their small pinions are elegantly variegated at the base, and adorned with the most delicate jet-

black feathers, which to the unassisted eye appear only like minute hairs, and yet are perfect feathers of the most exquisite description. They presently fly abroad, bearing with them seeds of equal rarity, with one minute groove fitted to another, and having a finished and elaborate mechanism whereby to facilitate the purpose for which they are designed.

Elizabeth Rowe loved the cyanus : that gifted woman who sought for it in her girlhood days, and obtained from the expressed juice a lasting transparent colour, little inferior to ultramarine, wherewith to paint some of her choicest flowers. And truly, as wrote the elegant author of *The Philosophy of Nature*, there was scarcely a flower, or an insect, or a bird, that grew, or crept, or sung in her garden, but yielded a source of pleasure. And so it will ever be if our minds are attuned aright, and we regard the universe as the temple of Him who fills all space, in which, as from one great altar, the incense of thanksgiving continually ascends.

Surely one might linger the whole day in a corn-field thus varied with flowers of all hues, from the bright Corn Marigold, or yellow Oxeye, to the pale-tinted Heart's-ease. "Mannour-courts do amerse careless tenants who do not weed out the former of these plants before it comes to seed," said good Master Threlkeld in the book which he compiled, "concerning things fitting to be known nearly two hundred years since." Wherefore ? Because the yellow oxeye (*Chrysanthemum segetum*) is extremely troublesome in the places of its sojourn, and difficult to eradicate. The farmer looks with a dissatisfied scowl over his field wherein this brilliant plant has fixed its abode. Not so the naturalist, and the lover of scenery; nor yet the moralist: the one acknowledges in his favourite corn-marigold a memorial plant, whose yellow flowers, following the sun with untiring diligence, teach him to look upwards with the eye of faith ; the other, in the brilliancy which is imparted to fields in tillage, the effect that is frequently produced, by means apparently inadequate; while the naturalist recognises a peculiarity of construction, which enables the marigold equally to sustain the heat of the summer solstice and the chill night winds of the waning year.

Saw you never, in cloudy and windy weather, with intervals of scorching sunbeams, when grain of every description ripens fast, some field on the slope of a hill-side of the most brilliant hue, as if the sun shone there exclusively—a lovely object amid the darkness of other fields, darkened with cloud shadows? That effect is produced by innumerable marigolds suffered to remain unmolested, or which have sprung up among the tender wheat, and from whence they could hardly be withdrawn. The Common Mustard (*Sinapis nigra*) also occasionally imparts somewhat of a similar appearance, being at least a foot and a half in height, and lifting its pale yellow petals to the full influence of air and light. It is, perhaps, scarcely necessary to observe, that the seeds, reduced to powder, produce the common mustard; that they yield a considerable quantity of expressed oil, which partakes but little of the acrimony of the plant; and lastly, that cataplasms, formed with crumbs of bread, vinegar, and powdered mustard-seed, are often applied as stimulants when required. All this is, perhaps, well known, but not the whimsical history attached to the name of this useful plant, which is as follows:—Philip the Bold, Duke of Burgundy, who lived towards the end of the fourteenth century, granted the town of Dijon armorial ensigns, with the motto, "*Moult me tarde*," which signifies, "I long, or wish ardently," and which, doubtless, had reference to some ungratified desire either of the duke or townsmen. However this might be, the arms and motto being sculptured over the principal gate, the middle word became effaced by some accident, and the merchant dealers in common sinapis-seed, intending to adorn their mustard-pots with labels of the city arms, copied the imperfect motto as it then remained, " *Moult tarde*," and hence the name of sinapis was changed into that of mustard, which it retains to the present day.

The Yellow Goat's-beard (*Tragopogon*), derived from two Greek words, a goat and a beard, which the down of the seed somewhat resembles, and *pratensis*, its specific name, is abundant in corn-fields, with the *T. parvifolius*, of which

YELLOW GOAT'S-BEARD, SCARLET PIMPERNEL.

the roots are esculent, and when cultivated in kitchen gardens for boiling or stewing, are called Salsafy. Both these species uniformly open early in the morning, and close their petals about twelve o'clock; they are consequently best known by the familiar appellation of "Go to bed at noon;"

and thus has a Dutch poet described the methodical life of
a tulip merchant, in allusion to these favourite plants :—

> "Oh! surely 'tis a bliss to lay one down
>   Upon a shady bank, where violet flowers
>   Smell sweetly, and the meads in blooming prime,
>   Till Flora's clock, the goat's-beard, marks the hours,
>   And closing, says—'Arise! 'tis dinner time;'
>   Then dine on pies and cauliflower heads,
>   And roam away the afternoon in tulip beds."

The remarkable property which is inherent in the yellow
and purple goat's beard, in the corn sow-thistle, mouse-ear,
hawk-weed, and scarlet pimpernel, with other solar flowers,
of thus unfolding their petals at an allotted time, and of
closing them again, and that most frequently before the sun
declines from the meridian, must be ascribed to an admirable
arrangement of spiral fibres.   Linnæus noticed this wonderful effect when in search of plants among the solitudes of
Lapland, and he gave to all such flowers the appellation of
solares; but it remained for modern botanists, among whom
the name of Ibbitson is conspicuous, to ascertain the cause
for such an extraordinary deviation from the laws of nature.

Spiral fibres must, therefore, be briefly noticed, that our
young friends may examine the subject for themselves when
they go forth into the fields during this pleasant month, and
observe that while some flowers spread abroad their petals
at noonday, others are beginning to enfold them.   These
fibres appear like fine cork-screw threads of a firmer texture
than the adjacent parts, and are readily distinguished by
carefully drawing asunder either a stem or leaf-stalk.   In
some small specimens, such as the pimpernel, they are
scarcely perceptible: in larger species they present an
elegantly-formed spiral, but in both they become firm and
rigid when no longer required.   By their ministry all the
operations of vegetable life that bear expressly on motion
are produced; flowers open in the morning and close at

night; leaves turn to the air and light, and a most beautiful effect is occasioned by the quivering of foliage in the wind; creeping plants also twine in their respective order, some, as already noticed, towards the west, others eastward. Heat and a strong light, in the first and second instances, produce a contraction of the spiral wires, and the slightest diminution of either, though unperceived by a looker-on, causes them to contract. 'Their form and position is likewise all important with regard to such flowers as remain expanded till eventide; by their agency the petals either shut or unfold—as, in mechanics, the same spring may be made to turn to the right or left in order to open or close a box.

The sweet and nutritious fruit of the yellow goat's-beard, if cut before the stems rise up, and boiled like asparagus, have nearly the same flavour: while those of the Strong-scented Lettuce (*Lactuca virosa*), which often grows beside it, yield an acrid and bitter juice that resembles opium, and possesses its narcotic qualities. An ancient poet, therefore, fabled, that Venus, when inconsolable for the loss of Adonis, threw herself on a bed of wild lettuces growing among classic shades, in the hope of obtaining sleep. The milky juice, when exuding in hot weather through the pores of the stem and leaves, is sufficiently tenacious to detain ants, and other small insects; and even in cloudy weather it is so exuberant as to ooze forth upon the touch of their light feet. Withering conjectures that its narcotic quality may sensibly affect the little wanderers, and incline them to sleep. One species, however, derives both food and shelter from the strong-scented lettuce; this is, the tiny *Livia lactucæ*, which journeys in and out unharmed either by the trap-like juice, or the overpowering scent. Thus admirably are all created beings adapted for the places to which they are assigned; but why so great a difference should be discoverable between two neighbour plants, rooted in the same soil, shone upon by the same warm sunbeams, and fertilised by the same showers, is a problem that none may solve.

These effects can alone be referred to the agency of a vital principle, though this all-pervading agency cannot explain them to our understanding; they are necessarily the result of chemical depositions and combinations, but we know not what these depositions and combinations are, nor yet the exciting causes, nor the laws that produce and regulate them. The root of the goat's-beard, in which the nutritious qualities are especially developed, is well deserving of brief notice. It is formed on the principle of a wedge, and penetrates readily into the earth; that of the wild lettuce, though somewhat similar, is also fibrous; each has an especial reference to the habits of the respective plants, and each has within it strongly coated vessels, by which they derive moisture from the earth.

The opening and closing of all flowers is consequently owing to internal mechanism of the most exquisite description, varying in different species, and, perhaps, somewhat more complex in such as the yellow goat's-beard, and strong-scented lettuce, time-pieces of Nature's making—which the weary ploughman often leaves his horses to look upon, and harvest-men love to sit beside when they rest from their work at noon.

Linnæus formed from such flowers an *Horologium Floræ*, or botanical clock. We recommend our young friends to occupy some of their leisure hours in the same way; taking note of different species which open at fixed times, and sketching them from nature; they will find, most probably, sufficient for their purpose on the borders of corn-fields and sunny banks. Thus beautifully has Mrs. Hemans referred to the botanical clock above-mentioned, and which is pleasingly associated with the memory of the Swedish naturalist :—

> " 'Twas a lovely thought to mark the hours,
>   As they floated in light away;
> By the opening and the folding flowers,
>   That laugh to the summer's day.

Thus has each moment its own rich hue,
    And its graceful cup or bell,
In whose colour'd vase might sleep the dew,
    Like a pearl in an ocean shell.

To such sweet signs might the time have flowed
    In a glorious current on,
Ere from the garden, Man's first abode,
    The glorious guests were gone.

Yet is not life, in its real flight,
    Mark'd thus—even thus—on earth,
By the closing of one hope's delight,
    And another's gentle birth?

Oh! let us live, so that flower by flower,
    Shutting in turn, may leave
A lingerer still for the sunset hour,
    A charm for the faded eve.''

Very dissimilar from that of the goat's-beard is the fibrous root of the elegantly-formed and slender *Agrimonia eupatoria*, or common Agrimony, generally found in corn-fields, and producing a graceful effect with its long terminating bunches of fine yellow flowers. This plant has also a specific use; the Canadians find an infusion of the leaves and flowers invaluable in burning fevers; it is likewise noticed as a specific for the jaundice. The Bladder Campion, or Spatling Poppy (*Silene inflata*), is associated neither with historic nor traditional remembrances, and yet, among such flowers as diversify a corn-field, what plant more singular in its construction or more deserving of close inspection! The calyx is purely white, and tastefully variegated with green or purple veins, inflated also like a gourd, and forming the most lovely clusters. Its relative, the Nottingham Catchfly (*Silene nutens*), on the contrary, recalls to mind many particulars of considerable interest. The generic name is given with reference to Nottingham, that neighbourhood being the first, and for many years the only place, in Great Britain where it was found; and the plant itself ranks fore-

most in local interest, not only on account of its beauty and
sweet evening scent, but for a singular viscid juice which
enwraps the stalk, and often imprisons small wandering
insects.

The original discoverer of this rare plant was T. Willisel,
one of the earliest and most industrious votaries of botanic
science. Ray subsequently noticed it, when he explored
the neighbourhood of Wollaton, nearly two hundred years
since, in company with his amiable friend and patron
Willoughby. The walls and rocks of Nottingham Castle
were beautifully mantled with the delicate flowers of the
catch-fly when the two friends visited them ; and since then
the cliffs at Sneinton Hermitage, about a mile eastward of
Nottingham Castle, are noticed as a second place of growth;
such also is the case at the present day, with the addition
of various huge masses of stone and excavations in Nottingham Park. The flowers begin to open in the second week
of May, punctually as when first observed by Willisel, and
continue for the space of six weeks, expanding most fully
towards eventide, at which time the petals bend slightly
downward, like those of the cyclamen.

Along the margin of fields also, and wandering some little
way among the corn, grow many " gently-breathing plants,"
with which grave herbalists and housewives cured in old
times the ailments of their neighbours—memorial flowers
also, by which old simplers commemorated worth or friendships, or neighbouring villagers associated the memory of
benefactors, whose skill or kindness might be shadowed
forth in the virtues of their favourite plants—such are Sweet
Marjorams, Cicélies, and Williams ; herbs Robert, Paris,
Bennet, Christopher, and Gerard, Timothy Grass, and Wild
Basil, with good King Henry—a small unobtrusive flower,
which aptly symbolizes the meekest and most unfortunate
of England's kings. The benefactors are long since departed;
the simplers and grateful villagers are gone ; the memory
of their loves and friendships, of their gentle virtues, who

they were, and why such names were given, are mostly past;
but the botanist likes to look on these memorial plants ; and
even the village matron, when she names or gathers them,
associates, though she cannot tell you why, a feeling with
those flowers which no other in the field or hedge-row can
elicit.

OCTOBER.

" WHERE are the songs of Spring ! Ah, where are they !
Think not of them : thou hast thy music too,
While Autumn clouds deck the soft dying day,
And touch the stubble plain with rosy hue."

OCTOBER is not, as it once was, a cold and cheerless month ;
nor even such as I remember it in my young days, when
chilling winds were much abroad, and storms of sleet were
seen at intervals careering across the hills. The botanist
still finds many of his favourite flowers growing profusely
along the borders of the fields, on stream sides, and on
hedge-banks, as if unwilling to depart. " Send us not
hence !" they seem to say, when, perchance, some stern
blast, herald of coming winter, rudely hurries past : and
when the scowling wind, as if forbad to do them harm,
goes howling on his way, and warm sunbeams break through
the clouds, how beautiful are they !—fragrant, too, and
cheering the heart of him who looks upon them with good
and comfortable thoughts. Wherefore ? Because they
tell him that he whose spirit's eye is fixed upwards, remains
unharmed amid the buffetings of this world's sorrows.

The Field Marygold (*Calendula arvensis*) is one such
flower. Its generic name, derived from *calendæ*, the first
of every month, aptly describes its almost perpetual flowering during the whole year, whenever a gleam of sunshine

visits its solitary growing-place, which is mostly on windy
eminences, such as Ballast Hill (Sunderland), or the shores
of Falmouth Harbour. This flower is also one of Flora's
watches, and notes the time of day in its own cheerless
haunts, where it often vegetates alone, or rather, in company
only with its kind. Yet, however desolate and bleak, thrifty
housewives adventure to its favourite habitats, because,
according to established authority, " no brothes are well
made without dryed marigoldes."

" Fair is the marigold, for pottage meet."

Simplers in old times held the flowers in great repute for
making cordials; and even at the present day the petals are
carefully picked, and kept preserved in casks, for the use of .
the apothecary. In England also, scarcely may you pass a
cottage garden without seeing tufts of marigolds among the
potherbs; and often do young children sit beside them, to
watch the gradual folding up of their yellow disks, when
the sun declines towards the west. " Mother," say they,
" father will soon come home, for the marigolds are going
to bed."

An emblem, it seems to me, of cheerfulness and punctuality
is this same flower; and yet .poets invariably connect
melancholy associations with the marigold :

" A symbol of my heart's sad grief,
 Of flowers the marigold is chief,"

sung one of the plaintive tribe in days long passed; and
modern poets, following his example, have poured forth
many a sad ditty in connection with this garden flower,
beloved of cottage dames and children, who care nought for
sentimental poets.

The Calendula has also been aptly termed *Solis sponsa*,
or Spouse of the Sun; and this with more propriety than
the " proud giant of the garden race," who is prevented

from folding up his petals by a peculiar rigidity of fibre, and which chiefly sustains his usual appellation from resemblance to the great luminary. The lowly marigold, though rather creeping on the ground than aspiring to eminence among her sisters, is so constructed as to shut up when many others remain open, and is thus elegantly described:—

> "This simple flower, that loves the sun,
> At his departure hangs her head, and weeps,
> And shrouds her sweetness up, and keeps
>   Sad vigils, like a cloister'd nun;
> Till his reviving ray appears,
> Waking her beauty as he dries her tears."

Shakespeare, in like manner, speaking of the marigold tribe, tells of them, that—

> "They sheath'd their light,
> And, canopied in darkness, sweetly lay
> Till they might open to adorn the day."

Though common to the corn-fields and vineyards of Portugal, and much valued as food for milch cows, and though spoken of as a favourite culinary herb in England by old simplers, the marigold has only recently been found growing wild in England. It is believed to have been first discovered at Falmouth, by B. Botfield, Esq.; and from the constant intercourse maintained between that place and Portugal it is extremely probable that the seeds were imported thence. Thus have various exotics been introduced, and, in process of time, become naturalized—as, for instance, several foreign plants now indigenous on Ballast Hill, near Sunderland, and in similar places: even the classic Acanthus, inseparably associated with Corinthian columns, has appeared in the mild climate of Penzance.

Of this the common Groundsel, mentioned in the January month, presents a familiar instance. Originally restricted to certain parts of Europe and the south of Asia, its seeds, brought with grain of various kinds into countries far remote, have now obtained a settlement throughout the world. The Canadian Fleabane (*Erigeron Canadense*), in like manner, opening with the groundsel, and continuing in flower till the present month, was first seen in the neighbourhood of Paris about a century since. Some traveller, returning to his native land, carried with him the seeds of this small plant, and these, readily vegetating, yielded flowers in abundance. From France the fleabane passed into England : its bristly seeds, adhering to the feathers of small birds, were borne beyond the precincts of the garden, where it formed a conspicuous ornament, and falling either on cultivated ground or heaps of rubbish, produced plants which soon came to be regarded as troublesome weeds. Husbandmen thus speak concerning them, but such is not the case ; they are extremely valuable for entrapping insects that resort to them during the summer months. Their leaves, interspersed with glands that secrete a glutinous fluid, attract and readily entangle small wayfaring creatures, whether winged or creeping ; and hence, in the south of Europe, it is customary to sprinkle the erigeron with the richest milk, in order still further to allure them. The English name is derived from its reputed power, when burned, of destroying those unwelcome visitants, whom no bulwarks can impede. The plant has other uses, among which one of the most prominent was stated by M. Lausanne to the Agricultural Society of Turin, viz., that the bark, after having undergone the process of soaking, may be manufactured into excellent paper.

Among memorial plants, and such as are endowed with singular properties, the Dutch Clover (*Trifolium repens*), though with little of outward beauty, is one of the most interesting. Its "day of pride" extends from May to September, and through the greater portion of the present month ; but wherever growing, its singular structure merits investigation. The flowers form a close head, standing up-

right, and delicately white: the calyx is greenish-white,
with purple streaks; and very pleasing is the effect produced
by a field of white clover, the resort of innumerable bees
and butterflies. When the sun declines in the ecliptic, and
the season of flowering is partly over, the globe-shaped
heads assume a peculiar appearance: the florets diverge from
the centre, spreading outwards and downwards, like an
umbrella, and form, most probably, a shelter for the ripening seeds. The species is remarkably sensible to atmospheric changes, and affords an excellent rustic weather-
glass, the leaves becoming relaxed in dry weather, but erect
when it is moist and rainy. Its spontaneous coming up
indicates good soil; and the richness of meadow and pasture
land is chiefly owing to the prevalence of trefoils, with
others of the same class.

Dutch clover has been already noticed as endowed with
singular properties: and most curious is the fact that if, in
the north of England, moorlands are turned up for the first
time, and strewed with lime, white clover appears in abundance; such also is the case in North America, a circumstance for which no satisfactory solution has yet been offered.
Ashes have likewise been found suddenly to augment the
growth of clover in places where it was scarcely observable;
and the wondering farmer has rejoiced in seeing its white
flowers creeping profusely on the ground, and forming a
pasturage on previously sterile places.

This same plant is also a memorial one: it is the national
emblem of Ireland, and claims a place in history, equally
with the rose and thistle which symbolize England and
Scotland. The Shamrock—for such is the name of the white
clover in the Emerald isle—is worn on the anniversary of
St. Patrick, and commemorates his landing near Wicklow,
in the beginning of the fourth century.

Chemistry reveals that the nutriment afforded by clover
contains a greater proportion of bitter, extractive, and saline
matter, than the proper grasses; and that when pure clover

hay is mixed as a fodder, it should be with summer growings,
rather than with the after-growth. The flowers of all the
species, when dried and powdered, may be made into bread;
and instances are on record proving that the inhabitants of
northern countries have been preserved from perishing by
their timely aid in seasons of scarcity. Different kinds
exhibit a striking exemplification of spontaneous movement
in vegetables: both leaves and flowers regularly follow the
course of the sun, and are sensibly affected by the approach
of storm-clouds. They may also be regarded as the hus-
bandman's weather-glass, uniformly contracting their leaves
when storms impend. Trefoils, with the exception of the
white clover, mostly pertain to the summer months; and in
some instances, the construction bears an obvious reference
to their place of growth. Of this the Bird's-Foot Trefoil
(*T. ornithopodioides*) affords a ready proof; the fibrous root
is furnished with small fleshy knobs, for the evident purpose
of resisting accidental drought during summer. The Sub-
terraneous Trefoil (*T. subterraneum*) presents a similar
deviation from the structure of plants in general. Observe
the strong, horny, stellated substance which grows from the
extremity of the fruit-stalk, stretching its rays, or white
thread-like filaments—resembling roots, which, however, do
not penetrate the earth—both outwards and downwards, and
enclosing and pressing the capsules to the ground, for the
purpose of partially burying them. Observe further, that
the seedlings are distinguished in winter by a pale and dark-
spotted pattern upon their leaves; and those who visit the
sandy waste below Folkstone church may study to advantage
this interesting plant, with its singular, stellated, floral
radicles.

Bees delight in the sweet-scented blossoms of the purple,
or Honeysuckle Trefoil (*T. pratense*), and extract much
honey from them. Few objects are more pleasing during
the end of the past month and the commencement of the
present, than a field thus visited with these busy and glad-

some insects, singing at their work. The true perennial Red
Clover abounds in the fertile grazing lands between Wain-
fleet and Skeyness, in Lincolnshire. Strange it seems that
a solitary cream-coloured specimen was discovered in a field
of purple clover belonging to Tracy Park, near Bath.

The unassuming family of *Bartsia* have few attractions
wherewith to interest the passer-by. The generic name was
given by Linnæus in honour of his beloved friend Barsch,
of Konigsberg, an ingenious young man of great promise,
devoted to the study of natural history, and who loved to
explore the wildest solitudes in quest of flowers ; the friend
also of Boërhaave, and deputed by him to pursue his
researches in Surinam. He died prematurely, in the flower
of his age, far from his native land ; having added another
victim to the many who, in all times, have been sacrificed
to an enthusiastic love of science. The yellow Viscid Bartsia
(*B. viscosa*) looks well in marshy places; as also the Alpine,
or Painted-cup (*B. Alpina*), of a deep purple violet colour,
which delights to dwell along the brink of rushing streamlets, on rough and stony banks open to the sun ; and is
nowhere more abundant than among rocks eastward of
Malghyrdy, in the Highlands of Scotland, and in Teesdale
Forest.

The Evening Primrose (*Œnothera biennis*) occasionally
frequents the same locality of streams and meads where
grows the Alpine Bartsia. And whereas the one dwells low,
and seems to shun the gaze of strangers, the other lifts up
her stately head, as if demanding the admiration of all who
pass. Condemn her not; the primrose has a work assigned
her which her lowly sister could not readily perform. When
evening closes in, she expands her pale yellow petals, holding
forth within them a " cup of paly gold" to all night wanderers: she loves to look the pale moon in the face, and
often in the witching hour of deep midnight, when stars
keep their watch on high, you may see the hospitable plant
surrounded by such insects as avoid the light of day—

warmly-coated moths, and beetles of various kinds, which resort to her for their nightly banquet. Associated with much of poetry, and many legends, this favourite flower grows luxuriantly, and attains to the height of several feet in a wild part of the Vale of Clwyd, on the road-side between Denbigh and Ruthlin, as also in many sites of historic interest in various parts of Britain. Botanists conjectured, therefore, that the seeds had been planted in old times, and that the evening primrose was rather of exotic than native growth. But the fact is otherwise; the beauteous flower

MEADOW SAFFRON, AND EVENING PRIMROSE.

has been discovered in such various and little-frequented spots, that no doubt remains as to her identity; growing at one time in some neglected cavity from which a coarse sand-stone had anciently been dug; at another, on storm-haunted hills and neglected fields, at a little distance from the sea; but nowhere so abundantly as in the Vale of Clwyd, with its rushing stream, and trees swaying in the wind, discovering, as the branches wave and bend the tower of old Ruthven in the clear cold moonbeams. Those towers look well when seen from the lone spot where grows the evening primrose; time has laid them waste, and the halls are roofless; the keep is a shapeless mass, and the massy walls are rent and torn, but no one could discover their dilapidated condition; and those who look upon them when slightly veiled by evening mists, might readily imagine that they still beheld that ancient fortress in all its pride.

Here, then, in one of the wildest parts of Denbighshire. the Evening Primrose unfolds her fragrant and large flowers. Often, too, when the nights are dark and sultry, and not the slightest breath of air is stirring, her petals emit a mild phosphoric light, and look as if illuminated for a holiday. Every part is consequently rendered visible; and he who does not fear to be alone in her wild and lonely growing place, may see a variety of nocturnal ephemera and insects hovering around the lighted petals, or sipping at the vegetable fountains; while others rest among the branches, or hurry up the stems as if fearing to be too late. The phosphorescent light thus kindled answers, without doubt, the purpose of a lamp, to guide the steps or flight of innumerable living creatures that love the night; and this is the more essential because flowers of all kinds are generally closed: not a single daisy is discoverable among the grass, search for them never so carefully—nor yet the numerous tribe of hawkweeds; the ample disk of the brilliant dandelion, which reflected the last rays of the setting sun, perchance from some high growing-place, is carefully folded up; and such bell-shaped flowers as are not susceptible of outward change become internally compressed, or else the nectar-holding cup is so guarded with rigid filaments, which answer the purpose of bars, that hardly can the most enterprising insect effect an entrance.

The Meadow Saffron, or tube-root (*Colchicum autumnale*), still lingers, with her sisters, beside our streams, in meadows open to the sun—the "orphan of year," which invariably announces the defoliation of trees, and which, like the infant in the poem of the Persian Sadi, smiles on the bosom of its dying parent, when resting on her couch of " sere and yellow leaves."

He who wanders somewhat sadly through the lanes, listening to gusty winds that chase the thistle down from out its covert in the brakes and hedges, often comes unexpectedly upon some green field where meadow saffrons lift their heads above the herbage. How cheerful-looking are they—how pleasant the thoughts of spring which they awaken ! and scarcely can the mind forego its illusion while gazing at them, so spring-like are those tube-roots. But higher thoughts than such as are awakened by opening leaves or buds rest on this orphan flower, which comes from out the earth beneath cloudy skies, and is often assailed by fierce winds, without a leaf or calyx, or even a protecting sheath like the green mantle of the snowdrop. Yet, still her beauty is renewed from year to year, and her light lilac-tinted petals stand unharmed, although the fields, her home, are white with frost, and pattering showers often descend on her defenceless head : nay, she will remain occasionally to beautify her companionless abode, from which all summer birds and flowers have departed, even when November has arrived with a train of clouds and storms.

NOVEMBER.

"' WE look abroad into the world, and see
But few familiar faces peeping forth
From hood or mantle.   Spring's bright flowery train,
And Summer's matron sisters, Autumn's, too,
Are mostly gone : yet, still in mead or glen
Linger some loved ones, smiling to the winds
That come and go, and hurry forth sere leaves
From out their haunts."

THOSE who walk in spring through fields where grows the
Meadow-Saffron, or Tube-root (*Colchicum autumnale*), may
see among the grass large capsules, or seed-vessels, somewhat egg-shaped, with three very blunt angles, surrounded
by several spear-formed leaves, which answer an important
purpose in the economy of the plant.

These egg-shaped capsules contain innumerable seeds;
they have been buried during winter at least ten or twelve
inches under ground, within the bulbous roots of the parent
flower; and they differ in this respect from such as pertain
to every other vegetable production. The reason for this
may be readily explained :—Flowers adorn the earth during
spring and summer; autumn has also her matron train,
which gradually recede before the chilling influence of frost,
and sharp east winds—all, excepting the meadow-saffron,
which looks cheerful, and seems to smile upon the fading
year, when even the hardy crane's-bill will scarcely linger
in our hedges. The seed-vessel, in all other plants, is
situated within the flower-cup, or just beneath it; but in
the colchicum a dissimilar instance is presented of that com-
pensatory system which supplies a deficiency in one part by
the perfection of another. The tube, which is seldom more
than a few tenths of an inch long, and adds considerably to
the beauty of flowers, extends in this plant down to the root;

the styles, also—those elegant and polished shafts, which uphold the yellow anthers, and in all cases reach the seed-vessel—are singularly lengthened for this purpose. Wherefore ? Because the plant blossoms late in the year, and would not, consequently, be able to ripen its seeds before the setting in of winter: this important office is therefore performed at a considerable depth below the earth, where neither rain nor frost can penetrate. The perfecting of the seeds, which in every other vegetable proceeds within a capsule exposed to the air, is here carried on during the dull months, when tempests are abroad, and snow often lies deep upon the ground. But then a new difficulty presents itself. Seeds, though capable of full development, cannot vegetate under ground ; they require the active ministration of concurring elements to call forth their latent qualities, and without such aid must be lost to the purpose for which they are intended. Behold, therefore, a second admirable provision, by means of which they are raised above the surface at an appointed season, and are rendered capable of being scattered in all directions. At first an angular and roundish green head emerges ; this gradually becomes developed, and a fruit-stalk is also visible, serving as a pedestal to uphold the capsule, which rises to the height of two or three inches. An important purpose is consequently attained by this uplifting of the vessel and its seeds from their dark growing place ; the seeds, in common with those of other plants, are exposed to the cheering sunbeams, and refreshed by passing showers. They ripen about, or rather before, the time of hay harvest, and speedily effecting their escape from out the capsule, which cracks in various parts, are dispersed by the wind—that random sower, which often bears them to a considerable distance. The order of vegetation, as regards the meadow-saffron, externally, is this :—The plant produces its flowers in September, its leaves and fruits in the following spring.

Thus all things act in concert for a prescribed purpose.

The Creator of the " orphan flower" wills that it should cheer the heart of man in its singleness and beauty, when nearly every flower has departed. But then the flower cannot perfect its seeds, and in no other way is its reproduction provided for ; a wonderful provision is consequently made for this purpose, causing him who looks upon it to rejoice, and to give thanks—to learn, perchance, a lesson of comfort, when no warbling voices of confiding birds, chanting from some leafless bough, tell him that, although having neither barn nor storehouse, they are cared for by Him who made them.

As respects the virtues of the colchicum ; the roots possess considerable acrimony, and when infused in vinegar, may be formed into a syrup, by the addition of sugar or honey, which is useful in coughs ; in this it resembles squills, but is less nauseous and acrimonious, though more sedative. Sir Everard Home submits, that this plant forms a principal ingredient in the celebrated French remedy, " Eau Medicinale," resorted to in paroxysms of the gout, but which proves destructive to the constitution of the patient.

As regards its baneful qualities, so virulent are their effects. that a single grain will produce the most injurious consequences ; even the seeds and flowers occasion violent symptoms, and the fingers have been benumbed while preparing them for medicine. From this deleterious quality in the beauteous meadow saffron, a useful lesson may be derived ; those also who pass through fields empurpled in autumn with its flowers, where sheep and cattle graze, may, likewise, in looking at them, gain instruction. The instinct with which those graminivorous animals are endowed prevents them from grazing on the tube-root : they shun

> " The baleful juice
> Which poisonous *Colchian* glebes produce."

Instances frequently occur of pastures being eaten down nearly bare, and the grass closely cropped, even under the leaves, but not a flower nor a leaf of this plant taken. Young calves, however, unmindful of warnings given, without doubt, by animals of more experience, have been killed by feeding on the leaves and capsules of the Colchicum in spring.

Gerard, when speaking of the Autumnal Saffron, or Crocus (*Crocus sativus*), says concerning it, " That pleasant plant that bringeth forth yellow flowers, was sent unto me from Robinus, of Paris, the painful and most curious searcher of simples." Hence it has been inferred that the autumnal saffron, which blossoms in September, and lingers in sheltered meadows, if the weather continue mild, even till the present month, was not originally indigenous. The seeds, like those of the fleabane already mentioned, were probably scattered beyond the precincts of the garden, and readily vegetated in neighbouring soils, extending to wilder parts and now growing as freely on the banks of the Derwent, as in the meadows of Saffron Walden.

The summit of the pistils, sometimes called chives, carefully collected, and moderately dried, are the saffron of the shops ; such as grow in England are preferred to any others, and are principally obtained from a considerable district in Cambridgeshire.

The season of saffron-gathering is replete with interest, and presents many a rural scene of exceeding beauty. Before the day has begun to dawn, and while as yet dew lies heavy on the grass and flowers, the busy cottagers, with their wives and children, are abroad in the saffron-fields ; they tread lightly, for fear of injuring the tender flowers, which they carefully collect and lay in baskets adapted for the purpose ; and these, when carried home, are soon emptied of their golden-tinted burdens, in some cool place—for the sunbeams may not look upon them, lest the moisture should exhale too quickly. The chives are then cautiously picked, and five or six pounds of the wet saffron generally yield one pound ; but the finest kind, or what is generally called hay-saffron, is not pressed into cakes, but merely dried. An acre of land, in favourable seasons, will produce, with good management, ten or twelve pounds of this valuable article, which has been held in high repute as a cordial, though little estimated in modern practice.

The earliest mention of the Saffron Crocus in this country occurred during the reign of Edward III., at which time its cultivation was successfully commenced. That enterprising monarch encouraged all attempts to promote industry among his subjects, and it is probable that the first growers of the saffron crocus experienced no small share of royal favour. Great difference of opinion seems, however, to have prevailed with regard to its efficacy. In the time of Henry VIII. the colouring of long locks of hair, called *glibbes*, as also various articles of dress, with saffron, was strictly prohibited; while in Ireland, according to the testimony of Lauremberg, the native women dyed their skirts with saffron, to preserve them from insects, and to add strength for their domestic or field-labours.

Artists who delight in the effects produced by strong contrasts in painting, and who therefore often introduce the scarlet cloak of olden days in their landscapes, would have equally admired the saffron-coloured garment of the Irish peasant. The rich tint afforded by the chives is indeed most beautiful; there is, perhaps, nothing analogous in nature, excepting the hue of morn, to which the poet has thus referred :—

> " How, when the rosy morn begins to rise,
> And waves her saffron streamer through the skies."

The Naked flowering Crocus (*C. nudiflorus*) belongs also to the British flora. This interesting fact was first clearly ascertained by the Rev. Mr. Beecher, of Southwell, Northamptonshire, by whom it was found in great profusion between Nottingham Castle and the river Trent, intermingled with the vernal crocus (*C. vernus*). It is distinguished from either of the preceding species by the segments of the summit being deeply sub-divided into from seven to twelve, though most generally nine, narrow linear tubes. The flowers, perfectly destitute of leaves, are in perfection during the past month, but often in mild weather embellish their solitary haunts till the beginning of November. The leaves begin to spring in December; they are more erect than such as pertain to the saffron and vernal crocus, the colour is considerably paler, and the ends are not decayed.

For those who like in autumn to seek out the habitats of such wild flowers as are assigned to bloom beneath her changing skies, we shall mention that the naked flowering crocus was discovered by Mr. Shepherd, curator of the Liverpool Botanic Garden, about a mile and a half from the town, on the road to Allerton; it grows, also, in pastures near Halifax; in the neighbourhood of Dudley; and in Pigwell and Lammas-fields, Warwick.

The Lattice Crocus (*C. reticulatus susianus* of Curtis's Magazine, p. 652), has been found growing wild by Dawson Turner, in Barton Park, Suffolk; the blossom is whitish, pale blue, or yellow; and its time of flowering, like that of the vernal crocus, is restricted to March, while the naked flowering and saffron crocuses belong to the autumn months.

Among such natural phenomena as continually excite attention, and are often wholly inexplicable, none are perhaps more wonderful than the different periods of flowering in such plants as pertain to the same family and are similarly constructed. No visible difference exists specifically in the vernal and autumnal crocus, and yet the one has never been known to flower except in March; nor can the latter be allured to throw open her beauteous saffron-tinted petals till the beams of the summer sun are past—

> " Say, what impels, amidst surrounding snow,
> Congeal'd, the crocus's flamy bud to glow ?

> Say, what retards, amidst the summer's blaze, .
> Th' autumnal bulb, till pale declining days?
> The God of Seasons, whose pervading power
> Controls the sun, or sheds the fleecy shower:
> He bids each flower his quickening word obey,
> Or to each lingering bloom enjoins delay."

Among the brotherhood of Scabious, the small, or lesser (*S. columbaria*) alone develops its bluish lilac flowers in ungenial weather. This is the more extraordinary, because the leaves and flowers are smaller than such as belong to the bitten and field scabious; and he who looks upon it might be ready to exclaim, " Surely this small plant must require the cheering influence of sunbeams and nursing dews, and, instead of hurrying winds, soft summer zephyrs as gentle playmates." Yet such are not assigned it; and the entomologist, watching beside this favourite flower for such as come, and go, and find a home among the five-cleft blossoms, will surely tell you that the mother butterfly, and the small *scabiosa*, though found upon the different species of wild scabious, must perish before their appointed time if this hospitable flower departed at an earlier period from our fields.

There was great joy beside a small lake on the road-side leading from Sconsar to Giesto, in the Isle of Skye, when, on a fine autumn morning of the year 1764, Sir John Macpherson, a distinguished naturalist, first discovered the rare and beautiful *Eriocaulon septangulare*, or Wreathed Pipewort, rising above the water;

> " He cared nought for wet or risk,"

but, leaping manfully from his horse, plunged into the lake, and brought forth his prize with no small exultation, as recorded in *Hook's Scotland*. About four years after, the plant was seen growing in different lakes of the same locality, though mostly in that of Loch-na-Caiplich, close to the road-side between Sligachan and Drynoch, and in such abundance that the white fibres of the roots were thrown upon the edges of the loch, as sea-weeds when deposited by the tide upon the shore.

Every part of the wreathed pipewort is singularly elegant; the roots are beautifully jointed, like those of a *conferva*, the stalk seven-angled, the leaves nearly transparent and full of cells; and the terminal head of flowers, with their purple anthers and curious scales, white petals and jet-black spots, are extremely attractive.

Associated, therefore, with the wild scenery and historic recollections of the Isle of Skye, with basaltic columns and lone lakes, and that memorial cave where, more than a hundred since, the Pretender and his faithful guide found an asylum for two days and nights, who may look upon the wreathed pipewort without feelings of the deepest interest!

The Water-Horehound, or common Gipsywort (*Lycopus Europæus*), is a pretty-looking flower, which chiefly affects sandy ground on the banks of streams and ponds; prized perhaps the more, because such flowers as charmed us in previous months have done their "day's tasks lovingly," and are mostly gone to rest beneath the earth.

Venture not alone, young botanist, into those wild and solitary places, where grows the water-horehound, remembering its cognomen of gipsywort, lest you should chance to meet with those "strolling people called gipsies, who," as wrote Threlkeld in years long passed, "do dye themselves of a blackish hue with the juice of this plant, the better with their tanned looks and swarthy skins to bubble the credulous and ignorant by the practice of magic and fortune-telling; they being in sooth a sink of all nations, living by rapine, filching, pilfering, and impostures."

Associations are widely different connected with the family of *Pyrola* or Wintergreen; of which the different members are chiefly found in places hallowed by records of old Time. They are all, with the exception of the serrated wintergreen (*P. secunda*) children of the spring or summer: but this fair plant, with its somewhat dense cluster of white fragrant and drooping flowers, belongs to September, and renders cheerful many a stream-side, or damp bank in woods, till the commencement of winter.

GIPSYWORT.

Neither artist nor poet is more influenced by local circumstances than the botanist ; and how much is the pleasure of a walk enhanced by the discovery of rare or beautiful plants amid spirit-stirring scenes—the elegant *pyrola,* for example, near picturesque ruins on the Wye, beside the venerable palace and monastery of Scone, or on the bank of the river Isla, with its rocks and headling waters tossing their billowy crests in wild career ; or by

"Roslyn's towers and braes sae bonny!
Craigs and water, woods and glen !
Roslyn's banks ! unpeer'd by ony
Save the muse of Hawthornden !"

DECEMBER.

"Love me well; I am the last of the sisterhood of months that you can love."—GILFILLAN.

KÄSTNER, the Hanoverian minister, whose talents are justly eulogized by the poet Hans Anderson, embodied in one of his flower-paintings a truly poetic thought. He introduced an arabesque of flowers, as emblematic of the flora of every season. It commenced with the crocus and snowdrop, the peeping nanny and pale primrose, succeeded by summer flowers; then came autumnal ones; and lastly, red berries and yellow-brown leaves, trophies wherewith December crowns his hedges and wild woods.

We have looked carefully along the banks, and in many a sheltered nook, hopeful to find at least some crane's-bill, or yellow oxeye—latest children of the year; but vain has been our search. Adopting, therefore, the idea suggested by the imaginative Kästner, we shall speak concerning the berries and brown leaves, and those elegant pensile tufts which hang like drapery on the autumnal hedges in profuse masses, enlivening the roadsides after flowers have long vanished; and remaining not unfrequently, in open weather, to the commencement of the present month.

Those tufts are formed by the Traveller's-Joy, or Virgin's Bower (*Clematis vitalba*), of which the stems extend from ten to twenty feet, and are covered in July, August, and September, with numerous sweet-scented flowers, which gradually give place to long, feathery, and downy seeds. "Travilcr's joie, is this same plant termed," says Gerard "as decking and adorning waies and hedges where people travell—*Virgin's bower*, by reason of the goodly shadowe which they make with their thick bushing and climbing, as also for the beautie of the flowers, and the pleasant scent and savour of the same; and, by country folks, ' Old man's beard,' from the hoary appearance of the seeds which remain long on the hedges."

This favourite creeper is common in the southern and western counties, especially in calcareous soil, and thrives even among rocks and loose stones, restricted, however, to certain localities: and, though growing abundantly in Gloucestershire, is rarely seen northward of Worcestershire, as remarked by Withering. The elegant profusion with which the traveller's joy ascends lofty trees, and even rocks, on the southern shore of the Isle of Wight, excites the admiration of every traveller. Those also who visit in autumn the Ballast Hills at St. Anthony's, and Wellington Quay, Northumberland, observe with pleasure the effect produced by its hoary seeds, when mantling the huge stones and hedges of its windy domicile. Few, if any, among our native plants are sufficiently prominent in their "autumn glory" to exhibit those changing hues, or lights or shadows, which are produced by clouds or sunbeams. Such, however, is the case with the Wild Clematis; and we have seen it under different aspects, reflecting the beams of the setting sun as if "tinged with a golden finger," or catching the cloud shadows as they come and go. Often, too, have we lingered with delight to observe the striking contrast presented by their silver tufts, and the clear blue of an autumnal sky, when partially veiling some high cliff, which rose precipitously from behind the road; or when, having covered the leafless branches of some wayside tree, the undulating clusters were seen waving in the wind.

The traveller's-joy has, like all plants, its own brief history inscribed on stems, and leaves, and flowers, that he who passes may read and take pleasure in the simple record. This, therefore, is its history; or rather, perhaps, the uses to which the different parts may be applied:—The branches are sufficiently tough to make bands for faggots or hurdles; and the whole plant is well adapted for covering arbours and rockwork in pleasure-grounds, being of rapid growth, and extremely hardy.   Field-mice avail themselves of the long feathery down attached to the seeds, to render their nests both warm and soft; and hence they are often found at the entrance to their holes.

> " For oft the little mouse
> Illudes our hopes, and, safely lodged below,
> Hath formed his granaries."

In France, the twigs are much used to make beehives and baskets; and those who occupy themselves with observing the wonderful arrangement and construction of vegetable tubes and air-vessels will do well to submit a branch or leaf of this interesting creeper to a common magnifying-glass.   Our village boys, however, know nothing of these curious facts: but having found out that air circulates freely through the stems, they cut a long stalk from some dry branch, which they light at one end; this done, they proceed to mimic the doings of grave men, who assemble on the village common beneath some old memorial tree, and, unmoved by poetic association or legendary lore, puff tobacco smoke through their long, unsentimental pipes.   Hence the country name of *smoke-pipe*, which is applied to the wild clematis.

Young naturalists often amuse themselves with placing a small cutting in some bright-coloured liquid, such as an in-fusion of saffron or cochineal, and observing how gradually the pores become filled.   The same effect is shown by the white hyacinth of our woods in spring; but in that case the transparency of the stem enables the progress of the coloured sap to be distinctly traced.

We have spoken in past months of the Black Briony, or Lady's Seal (*Tamus communis*), as ornamental to our hedges in May and June—that brilliant creeper, which terminates its long geographic range (from as far south as Algiers) on the north bank of the river Wear, above Sunderland.   The bright red berries look beautiful among the leafless branches, and beside them often gleam the equally red berries of the Wild Vine (*Bryonia dioica*), of which the root is sometimes formed into the human shape, by means of a mould adapted for the purpose, and sold for the *Atropa mandragora* of warm climates.

Look at the mournful Yew (*Taxus baccata*), springing from out the insterstices of some rocky acclivity, grasping the firm soil, and spreading forth its dark branches when all other trees are leafless. Methinks there is much of beauty in that stern evergreen, though poets and moralists speak only of its sable plumes; of cheerfulness, it may be—for what can equal in hue or form the bright cornelian berry that grows profusely on even the slenderest twig! Small birds resort in winter to the friendly yew as to an open banquet: they sing not those sad ditties which embody nought but moody feelings; their grateful songs are rather heard chanting the praises of One on High, who " careth for them," who has set the yew-tree often among wild rocks, and in stony valleys, where even the wild vine and lady's-seal can hardly find a rooting-place.

Why is it that poets will tune their harps to mournful numbers? Theirs is a glorious gift, that should gladden the hearts of those who hear them. They are the world's minstrels—their place is to lead the chorus of universal nature, which arises from grove and field and glen, and mountain, even when the yellow corn is gathered in, and sapless branches cast their summer suits ; when gusty winds wrestle with forest trees; and sunbeams, coming forth as if by chance, shed a wayward light on meads and waters; when, too, the nights grow cold and long, and sleety storms career athwart a wintry sky—there is still much of gladness left, ay, of pleasant sights; why, else, these beauteous berries that shine along the hedges—not brown nor grey, but of the brightest tints, that wayfaring birds may readily discern them ?

And low upon the ground grow many simple plants of
equal brilliancy, as if to cheer the hearts of those who pass
through miry ways. The Scarlet Cartilaginous Helvena
(*H. cartilaginea*) peeps forth from amid tufts of moss, or on
old weedy walls and rocks, in company with lichens of all
shapes and tints, associated with many a spirit-stirring tale
of bygone days, and delighting the youthful botanist who
climbs fearlessly to some giddy height in order to obtain
such a novel prize. In like manner, the Scarlet Conferva
(*C. coccinea*) equally affects both rocks, and stones, and
fuci, within reach of the wild waves' play; and the bright
Red-cup Lichen (*L. cocciferus*) holds forth its slightly hol-
lowered cups, edged with beautiful scarlet tubercles, on lone
heaths, when even the hardy fern looks brown and withered.
You may hear the voices of young children calling eagerly
to one another, when they first discover the Scarlet Peziza
(*P. coccinea*) on decayed sticks in woods, and on damp
hedge-banks where streams ooze forth; or else its pale
orange relative (*P. punicea*) on old walls, or lichen-dotted
branches which the winds of autumn have broken from
some near tree.

Listen to what old Gerard wrote, more than three centuries
since, concerning the Arum, Cuckoo-pint, Wake-robin, or
Lords and Ladies (*A. maculatum*)—for by such dissimilar
names is this singular plant designated; and if you have
not already sought for it in shady places, ditch-banks, and
rough grounds, go forth while yet there is time, and you
cannot fail to find the arum, for its scarlet berries embellish
many a lone haunt when flowers are no more and even its
own foliage has long since disappeared.

" This plant," said the prince of herbalists, " hath great,
large, smoothe, shining, sharp-pointed leaves, spotted here
and there with blackish spots, mixed with some blewnesse,
among which riseth up a stalke nine inches long, besprinkled
with certain purple spots. It beareth also a certaine long
hose, or hoode, in proportion like unto the ears of a hare,

in the middle of which hoode cometh forth a pestle, or clapper, of a murry, or pale purple colour, which being past, there appeareth in place thereof a bunch or cluster of berries, in manner of a bunch of grapes, greene at the first, but after they be ripe, of a red, like coral, and full of juice: wherein lie hid one or two little hard seeds. This hooded plante do differ according to the varieties of countries, being sharper and more biting in some than others. Travellers relate that in the northern partes, bears, after they have lien in their dens without any manner of sustenance, doe, as soon as they come forth, eat the cuckoo-pint."

Men in old times were ready to believe whatever travellers were pleased to relate; the fact, however, concerning the shaggy occupants of Scandinavian forests is by no means improbable. The qualities of the root are both nutritive and farinaceous, and Widelius conjectures that the plant named Chara, on which the soldiers of Julius Cæsar made a sort of bread at Dyrrachium during a scarcity of provisions, was either this species of arum, or one much resembling it. We may, therefore, naturally conjecture that the bear, when first awaking, seeks for such roots or vegetables as are best adapted to supply his wants. Thrushes, in like manner, often in winter repair to places where the arum grows, and scatch off the snow, in order to obtain the warm and pungent roots. Is this an act of memory, or of instinct? Does the warbling thrush, when singing to his mate in spring, observe the stemless arum, with its large glossy leaf, and purple, or buff-coloured spike, and mark its place of growth, with reference to coming winter? or does an exquisite sense of smell enable him to discover it when the ground is covered with snow?

The arum has apparently no assigned locality; but it grows most profusely in Portland, flourishing even upon stubble lands, and producing a singular effect.

Those who visit that island somewhat late in the season, and after the leaves decay, may observe a number of women engaged in digging up the roots for the supply of London dealers, who use it as a substitute for the Maranta, or Indian arrow-root. Great care is, however, requisite, to dissipate the acrimonious quality of the root, by repeated washings, or soakings in hot water. Many hundred-weight are sold annually at Weymouth for starch, or as food for young children and invalids ; and some naturalists relate that a sufficient quantity might be collected from the Flat Holmes to furnish a considerable article of commerce.

> " The woods are stripp'd with the wintry winds,
>   And faded the flowers that bloomed on the lea ;
> But one lingering gem the wanderer finds,
>   'Tis the ruby fruit of the wild-brier tree!
>
> " The strong have bow'd down, the beauteous are dead ;
>   The blast through the forest sighs mournfully ;
> And bared is full many a lofty head ;
>   But there's fruit on the lowly wild-brier tree !
>
> " It has cheer'd yon bird that, with gaudy swell,
>   Sings, ' What are the gaudy flowers to me ?
> But here will I build my nest, and dwell
>   By the simple, faithful, wild-brier tree ! ' "

Truly, the little bird does wisely who builds her nest in the wild-brier tree (*Rosa canina*). The long, trailing, and overarching branches, well armed with large hooked prickles, form impregnable citadels against the attacks of prying school-boys searching for nests. The cat too, who, leaving her master's cottage, prowls through the neighbouring fields in the beautiful nights of May and June, dares not venture within its precincts. Thus, well defended and surrounded with those blossoms, from which a perfumed water may be distilled, infinitely more fragrant than such as is extracted from garden roses, sings on the grateful bird, to cheer his mate while sitting on her nest; and when the quaking trees are forced by stormy blasts to wrap themselves in suits of mossy frieze, a banquet is prepared by the same hospitable tree for the support of the tender household, who first trilled their songs of duteous thanks beneath her branches. And not for them only: innumerable birds are sustained during winter by such berries as grow upon our hedges and in the woods.

In such wild haunts the Mountain-ash (*Pyrus accusaria*) also displays his beauteous clusters of ripe berries in mountainous and boggy places. Vestiges of ancient superstitions are associated with this tree: and still the natives of North Wales adorn their houses with its branches, in remote and isolated districts, as preservatives against all spells and grammarie—a custom derived most probably from Druidic times; for no where does the mountain-ash, or roan, as it is termed in Scotland, grow more abundantly than among the circles of unhewn stones in places where the Druids haunted. In one part of the Highlands, at Strathspey, sheep and lambs are made to pass through a hoop of roan-wood on May-day; and the Scottish dairymaid uniformly drives her cattle to the shealings, or summer pasturages, with a rod from her favourite tree.

We will now enumerate some of the wild plants more or less poisonous, and which are largely used for medicinal purposes.

POISONOUS WILD PLANTS.

HELLEBORE.

THE name Hellebore is of Greek origin, coming probably from *elein* to seize, and *bora*, in eating, and it is very appropriatley applied to certain plants of the natural order *Ranunculaceæ*, which are remarkable for their deleterious properties. The Black Hellebore (*Helleborus niger*), commonly known as the Christmas Rose, is one of the few plants which blossom in our gardens in winter. It is an irritant poison, although sometimes given medicinally; its properties are those of a hydragogue-cathartic, that is, producing watery evacuations. It has been found useful in apoplexy, amenorrhœa, epilepsy, dropsy, hypochondriasis, and cutaneous diseases; it is now seldom prescribed, and certainly ought never to be given, except under the direction of a medical practitioner. The dose of the powdered root is from 5 to 10 grains, of the extract the same; of the tincture 1 drachm.

The above species is not indigenous to this country, but there are two plants of the genus which are, viz.—the Green Hellebore (*H. viridis*), which is not a common wild flower with us, but may be found occasionally in woods and thickets on a chalky soil. It grows to the height of about a foot and a-half, has long serrated leaves, a round erect stem, and forked branches; the blossoms, which appear in April or May, are not unlike those of the Christmas rose in shape, but differ from them in colour, being of a dark green, paler, and strongly veined on the under side. The plant has been employed in America as a remedy for fevers of the typhoid class, and for some convulsive diseases of children ; it is, however, a dangerous remedy, and one that had better be left alone. The other native species is the Stinking Hellebore (*H. fœtidus*), which is not uncommon on chalky lands, in woods and hedges, and may sometimes be seen in our gardens with the earliest flowers, expanding its pink-edged globular blossoms at the extremity of the thick succulent stems, sometimes two feet high; the leaves are numerous, long, and narrow, with serrated edges, and of a full rich green colour, which they retain throughout the winter. The whole plant exhales a fœtid odour, and is so extremely poisonous, that it is quite unsafe to allow it to grow in gardens to which children have access. Notwithstanding this, however, it was once a favourite medicinal herb ; and in Yorkshire and Westmoreland it is still given for worms and other maladies incidental to children, and the leaves have been eaten with bread-and-butter, and in several instances have proved fatal. The plant grows very abundantly in Westmoreland, where it is termed Felon Wood, a name also applied to the common Nightshade ; not, probably, as some writers have thought, on account of its evil qualities, but because it has been used for the cure of whitlows—a popular name for which in some parts is "felon." Old medical writers recommend the plant for jaundice, gout, and convulsions, and sometimes call it Stinking Bear's Foot: the root and the dried leaves are given, but the former is the most powerful ; the dose is from 5 to 20 grains ; of the decoction, made by boiling a drachm of the leaves in 8 ounces of water, a fluid ounce is the common dose.

The White Hellebore (*Viratrum album*) belongs to a different order of plants, the *Melanthaceæ*, or Colchicum family ; this is violently emetic and cathartic, and will sometimes cause great pain and purging of the bowels, if applied externally to a wound or ulcer; sniffed up the nostrils, it causes much irritation and sneezing; it was, therefore, like the other Hellebores, formerly used as a sternutary or sneezing-powder, being considered, when used in this way, a remedy for headache, bad eyes, and disorders of the brain. The ancients considered Hellebore a cure for madness, and they had a popular saying—"Send the madmen to Anticyra," an island in the Gulf of Corinth, where the plant grew plentifully. The soothsayers of old used Hellebore in their incantations, and they professed to believe that it had power to drive away evil spirits, therefore they scattered it over their dwellings, with certain mysterious rites and ceremonies. Burton, in his " Anatomy of Melancholy," alludes to this superstition of the Romans thus :—

> " Borage and Hellebore fill two scenes;
> Sovereign plants to purge the veins
> Of melancholy, and cheer the heart
> Of those black fumes which make it smart.
> To clear the brain of misty fogs,
> Which dull our senses and soul clogs :
> The best medicine that e'er God made,
> For this malady is well assayed."

NIGHTSHADE.

The Deadly Nightshade, whose botanical name is *Atropa Belladonna*, belonging to the natural order *Solanaceæ*, is a very poisonous plant. It is not uncommon in the hedges in some parts of England; it has a purple, bell-shaped blossom, about an inch long, and oblong pointed leaves, growing on short stalks, generally in pairs; the stem is upright, stout, and rather hairy, sometimes altogether geeen, but oftener tinted with red: the berries are about the size of wild cherries, of a dark purple colour, glossy, sweet, and not unpleasant to the taste; hence they have been often eaten by children, ignorant of their deleterious qualities, with fatal results. *Belladonna* means literally Fair Lady, and was most likely given to this plant on account of the tempting appearance of these berries: *Atropa* refers to its deadly properties, coming from *Atropos*, the ancient name of one of the fates, or evil destinies. The Saxons called the plant *Banewort*, or *Murdering weed*. *Raging* and *Furious*

Nightshade are also old names, significant of its evil character. It was likewise called *Dwale*.

The leaves, roots, and berries, indeed every part of this plant, are powerfully narcotic, and act in some cases as a diaphoretic, diuretic, and laxative. Medicinally it is em-

ployed to alleviate pain, great nervous excitement, and
spasm; it is also useful in neuralgic and convulsive affections, as well as in rheumatism, dysmenorrhœa, &c. Its
powerfully poisonous nature, however, renders great caution
necessary in its administration; and it should never, on any
account, be resorted to by unqualified persons. Dryness
and constriction of the throat, dimness of sight, and giddiness, are the symptoms of the necessity for its discon-
tinuance. The following are its officinal preparations, with
their doses:—Powdered leaves, 1 grain once or twice a day,
gradually increased to 2 or 3 grains, under careful super-
vision; the powdered root is sometimes used—it is thought
to be rather stronger; from 1-8th to 1-4th of a grain is the
dose for children. Extract, from 1-4th to 1-8th of a grain
twice a day; for a child, 1-12th of a grain; Alcoholic Extract, from 1-6th to 1-4th of a grain; Tincture, from 5 to
20 minims, equal to from ½ grain to 2 grains of the dried
leaves; Atropine and Sulphate of Atropine, from 1-30th to
1-6th of a grain; this is the active principle of Belladonna,
and is seldom given internally in this country.

For external use it is employed in the form of cerate,
cataplasm, liniment, lotion, oil, plaster, solution, ointment.
The vapour of the decoction is sometimes inhaled to relieve
asthma, and the extract is applied to relieve pain, and dilate
the pupil of the eye.

The poisonous **nature** of this plant has been long known;
thus, we read that the Scotch, under Macbeth, having
defeated the **army** of the Danes under Sweyn, destroyed
many of them by mixing its juice with ale, wine, and
bread. Earlier yet, we have it recorded by Plutarch, that
the soldiers of Mark Antony were drawn by hunger to eat
unknown herbs, and the camp became filled with unhappy
restless men, who, one by one, died of the poison, which
was, no doubt, that of Belladonna. In more modern times
we have it recorded, that 150 soldiers were poisoned by this
plant near Dresden. Its first effects appear to be a pleasant

state of mental exhilaration, which, however, is soon succeeded by corresponding depression, such as all vegetable
narcotic poisons produce. A strong emetic of sulphate of
zinc, about 30 grains, in warm water, every 20 minutes or
so, should be given in a case of poisoning by this plant,
unless the stomach-pump can be rendered available. After
this, strong coffee, or sal-volatile, or brandy, to counteract
the depressing effects.

Nearly allied to the plant we have been describing is the
Woody Nightshade or Bitter Sweet, the *Solanum Dulcamara*
of botanists, belonging also to the natural order *Solanaceæ*,
the dried twigs of which are sometimes used medicinally,
being regarded as alterative, diuretic, sudorific, and mildly
narcotic; it is used in skin diseases and catarrhal affec-

tions; also in scrofula, chronic rheumatism, and syphilis; the dose being—of the powder, from 1 to 3 scruples; of the decoction, about a wineglassful; of the extract, from 5 to 10 grains; of the syrup, half an ounce to an ounce. This plant is nearly allied to the potatoe, which it very closely resembles in the odour of its root. It grows wild with us in roadside hedges, and especially affects those near ponds or streams of water; its twining stems often reach to the height of five or six feet; it has purple and yellow blossoms, and bright scarlet berries; and children are said to have been poisoned by eating the latter; as have grown persons from an overdose of the decoction of the fresh twigs, which, in the country, are still extensively used. For making the decoction, the twigs should be gathered whenever as thick as a goose-quill; 1 ounce of them, chopped up, to be boiled in a pint and a half of water, until reduced to half the quantity. There are, however, many safer and better remedies. We give a cut of the plant (p. 115) for comparison with that of its more poisonous relative.

ACONITE.

There are several species of Aconites, all highly poisonous; the roots of some which grow on the lofty pastures of the Swiss mountains were formerly powdered and mixed with food to form a bait for wolves; hence the first of the above names. That which produces the most virulent poison is the *Aconitum ferox*, which is a native of India. Of the kinds grown in our gardens—including the Yellow Monkshood (*A. anthora*), and the Hairy Wolf's-bane (*A. barbatum*)—the Purple Monkshood (*A. napellus*), called by the old English writers the Purple Helmet-flower, is the most common. Its tall spike of dingy purplish blossoms is very conspicuous during the summer months, but children and persons in delicate health should beware of approaching it too near, as even <u>inhaling</u> the scent has been known to produce sickness and fainting. Many lamentable accidents have occurred through mistaking the roots of the Aconite for Horse-radish, and this should be a sufficient reason for excluding the former plant, from the kitchen garden at all events.

The Aconite belongs to the natural order *Ranunculaceæ;* it is, therefore, nearly allied to the buttercup of our fields and the ranunculus of our gardens; the leaves and roots are the parts of the plant employed in medicine. In proper doses they are anodyne, sedative, diuretic, and diaphoretic ; they are administered in dropsy, consumption, hypertrophy, or excessive growth of the heart, &c.   Outwardly they are used to relieve neuralgic and rheumatic pains, the best form of application being a liniment as follows :—Extract of Aconite, 1 scruple ; Soap Liniment, and Compound Camphor Liniment, of each 1 ounce ; rubbed into the part affected night and morning.   It is sometimes used in the form of ointment, of which there are two formulas in the Pharmacopœia, the simple and the ammoniated, the latter being the preferable.   The dose of Extract of Aconite is from a $\frac{1}{4}$ grain up to 2 grains ; that prepared according to the Edinburgh Pharmacopœia is considered the strongest ; of the Tincture of Aconite there are three strengths—London dose 7 to 10 minims ; Dublin, 5 to 8 minims ; and that called Dr. Flemming's, 3 to 5 minims.   In prescriptions it should be specified which of these is meant.   There is also the active principle of Aconite called *Aconitine,* which is far too powerful for internal use ; it is sometimes ordered for ointment ; the price of it is extremely high.   5 grains mixed with 1 ounce of lard makes a very strong ointment.

Aconite, Poisoning by.—*Symptoms.*   A burning sensation in the throat, pain in the abdomen, vomiting and diarrhœa, succeeded by giddiness and delirium, which end in coma and convulsions, if enough has been taken to cause death.

Treatment.   Vomiting to be produced by mustard, salt, a feather down the throat, or the readiest means, and encouraged by copious draughts of thin gruel or warm water, adding a little spirit, or wine, if the depression be extreme ; in which case also apply hot mustard and water to the extremities, and place large mustard plasters down the spine to rouse the nervous system.   Promote the evacuation of the bowels by repeated doses of castor-oil given in hot brandy and water, should they not act very freely without, and administer 15 drops of spirits of sal-volatile in camphor mixture about every hour, when the poison is ejected, and the patient appears to be recovering.

HEMLOCK.

The common Hemlock (*Conium maculatum*) is one of the handsomest of our native umbelliferous plants; it has large deeply indented leaves, and hollow shining stems, sometimes measuring as much as three inches round at the base; they are marked with purplish red spots, by which this plant may be readily distinguished. The lower leaves, which are on long concave footstalks, are larger than the upper, and of a paler green. The small white blossoms appear in June and July. The whole plant, which sometimes attains the height of four or five feet, is faint and sickly, coming out most strongly when the leaves are bruised. The fibrous root is about as thick as the finger, and smells exactly like parsnip.

In the Spotted Hemlock, as it is sometimes called, there resides a powerful narcotic poison, this principle being most abundant in the leaves and seeds; it is common in many English counties; and is believed to have yielded the State poison of the ancient Greeks, by which Socrates and others were put to death. The roots are said to have, when boiled, very much the taste of parsnips; but we should not recommend any of our readers to make a meal of them, as it is likely that, in certain states of the atmosphere, or conditions of growth, they too may be poisonous. Conium, as the plant is called medicinally, is given as an anodyne, antispasmodic, and deobstruent; in scirrhous and cancerous diseases it acts as a palliative; also in pulmonary irritation, hooping cough, neuralgia, chronic rheumatism, and all cases in which sedatives are likely to be of service; in skin diseases and enlarged viscera, too, it is given, and several other diseases.

The dose of the leaves, dried and powdered, is 2 or 3 grains, gradually increased until slight nausea or giddiness is produced; of the Extract, from 2 to 3 grains, once a day, increased as above; of the Compound Pill, from 3 to 5 grains two or three times a day; Tincture, from 20 to 40 minims. There are two other preparations of this plant, but they are very rarely employed. The ointment and plaster are anodyne and resolvent, and the dried leaves, mixed with a carrot or other poultice, and applied twice a day, corrects

the fœtor of a cancerous discharge in a very short time, and alters the discharge into a salutary pus.

The activity of Conium is much diminished by acids; hence, in a case of poisoning by this plant, vinegar would be a good and easily-procured remedy; of course, the stomach should be relieved of as much of the poison as possible by emetics. As a proof of the poisonous nature of the plant, we may mention that, during the present year, a boat's crew of men from H.M.S. "Wellington," while on shore at Cambeltown, dug up a quantity of Hemlock, which they mistook for wild celery, or parsley. The men who partook of it—eight in number—became very ill, and two of them died. Several of our wild plants which produce

these blossoms in umbels are of a poisonous nature, such as the Lesser Hemlock, or Fool's Parsley (*Æthusa sinapium*). It may be found almost in every dry situation; grows to the height of from one to two feet, and has altogether a lighter appearance than the species first described; a slight reddish

tinge may be noticed at the lower part of the stem, and there
is one very obvious peculiarity attached to the blossom;
beneath each small cluster is a partial umbel, having three
slender leaflets all on one side, that are scarcely thicker
than threads, and about the third of an inch long.   This is
sometimes called Dog's Parsley, and serious consequences
have ensued from the garnishing of dishes with the leaves

in mistake for the real parsley; the knobs of the roots have
also been eaten by children for turnips with fatal results;
this root, however, has a strong acrid taste, and the whole
plant when crushed so unpleasant an odour, that one won-
ders how it can ever have been eaten. The symptoms of
poisoning by it are nausea, vomiting, spasmodic pain, numb-
ness, &c.

Another common member of the natural order *Umbelliferæ* is the Hemlock Water Dropwort found in moist places; it has a large hollow stem from two to four feet high, and puts forth its yellowish white blossoms in globular clusters in July. The scientific name of this plant is *Œnanthe crocata ;* it is considered by some the most deadly of our native vegetable poisons, and to be equally fatal to man and the inferior animals. Many deaths are recorded to have taken place from eating the roots by mistake for those of the Water Parsnip: they are not disagreeable in taste, to deter persons from doing this. The saffron-coloured, milky juice which the whole plant discharges, wherever bruised or broken, and especially at the root, is a sure indication of its poisonous nature; every plant which has this peculiarity should be avoided. In some localities where it is found, especially in Pembrokeshire, the plant is known by the popular name, "Five-fingered Root." It is said to be useful in cutaneous diseases; applied to the skin it produces redness and irritation. The symptoms of poisoning by it are inflammation of the stomach, with great cerebral disturbances, indicated by giddiness, convulsions, and coma.

HENBANE.

The botanical name of this plant is *Hyoscyamus niger*, derived probably from the Greek *yos*, a hog, and *kyamos*, a beast, so named either because hogs eat it, or because it is hairy, like swine ; by some it is called Hogbean, *Faba suilla*. It belongs to the natural order *Solanaceæ*, and is a strong narcotic poison, the leaves and seeds being chiefly used for medical purposes ; the latter are the most active. There are two cultivated varieties of this plant, one annual and the other biennial ; the latter is considered the most active. In this country the plant grows wild on waste and ruinous places ; it appears to prefer a chalky soil, and is sometimes found on cliffs by the sea-side; it is commonly about three feet high, with a hairy stem, and large deeply-indented leaves of a dull, sickly-looking green. It béars, from June to August, dull yellowish white blossoms, thickly marked

with purple lines; it has a peculiarly fetid and unpleasant odour. Notwithstanding Pliny's dictum that "all Henbane is of the nature of wine, and is therefore offensive to the understanding," this plant is much used in modern medical practice, as it is found to allay pain, and subdue nervous excitement, without confining the bowels, and acting otherwise prejudicially, as opium often does: in irritable affections of the lungs, bowels, and other organs, its sedative properties render it extremely valuable. The dose of the powdered leaves is from $\frac{1}{2}$ a drachm to 2 drachms; of the fresh juice expressed and preserved, from $\frac{1}{2}$ a drachm to 1 drachm; of the tincture, $\frac{1}{2}$ a drachm to 2 drachms; of the extract (the most common form of administration), from 2 to 10 grains. There are also Cataplasms, Plasters, and Oil of Hyoscyamus, intended for external use. In over doses, Henbane causes delirium, coma, and death, and its operation is in general very rapid.

The seeds sometimes relieve toothache; the best method of use, for this purpose, is to heat a small piece of metal nearly red-hot, and placing them on it, let the fume which arises ascend into the open mouth; taking care not to inhale too much of it.

Children sometimes play with the capsules of the Henbane. Clare alludes to this, and, speaking of himself, and of his young companions, says—" we christened them our ' loaves of bread;' " this, however, was very dangerous play, for although the seeds have less of the narcotic property than the rest of the root, yet they have sufficient of it to produce very alarming results; a few of them, according to Lightfoot, have deprived a man of his reason and the use of his limbs, and Sir Hans Sloane records the case of four children who, having eaten some of the capsules in mistake for filberts, exhibited all the symptoms of narcotic poisoning; continuing for two days and nights in a profound sleep.

ARUM.

The common plant of the hedges, called "Lords and Ladies" by the country people, is the Spotted Arum (*A. maculatum* of botanists); it belongs to the natural order *Araceæ*, and is sometimes known as Wake-Robin, or Cuckoo-Pint; it was formerly called Starchwort, because the starch procured from the roots was used for stiffening ruffs; has large glossy halbert-shaped leaves, with purplish black spots, and a tall pale green sheath, which opens about May, and displays a

column of yellowish-green, with a spike of a brownish-red; these the country children term " Lords and Ladies." By about the end of August, a cluster of scarlet berries may be seen to crown the top of the naked stalk; glowing in the sunshine, they look very tempting, but are highly poisonous,

as are also the leaves, and, indeed, every part of the plant,
the fresh juice of which is so irritant that it will blister the
skin, as will, also, slices of the root; and yet Culpepper,
following other old writers on medicinal herbs, recommends
the juice as an antidote against poison or the plague.

A nutritious farina may be obtained from the root by
drying it in the sun, powdering, and then repeatedly washing.
It used to be sold under the name of "Portland Sago,"
much of it being prepared in the island of Portland, where
the plant was very plentiful. A celebrated Parisian cosmetic,
called "Cypress Powder," is also made from the Arum root.

The *symptoms* of poisoning by this plant are swelling of
the tongue, constriction of the muscles of the throat, so
as to prevent swallowing; tremor, rigidity of the limbs,
and sometimes violent convulsions. For *remedies*, the
stomach-pump and emetics, with other means advised to
counteract the effects of vegetable irritants.

BRYONY.

Of the Bryonies, there are two species common to this
country; they are both graceful and handsome plants, and
similar in their mode of growth, in which they resemble the
hop and the honeysuckle; they are, however, easily distinguished from these familiar plants, and also, by an
observing eye, from each other, by certain obvious charac-
teristics. The Red-berried Bryony, called by botanists
Bryonia Dioica, has large palmate leaves, which, in early
spring, have a greyish tint; but as the summer advances,
they become of a rich full green colour, and are covered on
both sides with prickly hairs. The blossoms, which are of
a greenish white, veined with darker lines, expand in May,
springing three or four together from the angle beneath the
leaf and stem. In autumn their place is occupied by
clusters of green berries, which assume, as the season ad-

vances, a deep-red colour ; they are smooth, but not glossy, and remarkably round in form. The leaves of this species have in autumn a slight musky odour.

This species is found most abundantly in the southern counties of England ; it has a large root, of a dirty yellow colour, which penetrates deeply into the soil. It was

formerly recommended as an application for whitlows and other eruptive diseases ; water distilled from it was employed as a cosmetic to remove freckles, &c. ; wine or spirit in which it had been steeped was taken for dropsy and other maladies, as was also an infusion. It is a very unsafe medicine, being extremely irritant, as are the juicy berries of the plant, although not so poisonous as those of the White Bryony, botanically named *Tamus communis,* which is popularly called Tetter Berries, Wild Hops, Wild Nip, and Wild Vine. This, like the last species, is a very ornamental plant, wreathing its graceful festoons about our hedges and woodland trees; it may be known from the other kind by its glossy heart-shaped leaves and small green blossoms. In September these leaves have a purplish or yellow hue, and then it is that the clusters of large green berries appear on the stems; in October, these ripen into a bright scarlet hue, and look very tempting; they are violently emetic, and eaten in any quantity are likely to cause death. This is a plant which was formerly held in considerable repute for its medicinal virtues; it has roots of immense size, sometimes as much as two feet long and as thick as a man's arm. They are white, succulent, and fleshy, with a bitter, acrid, and disagreeable taste; when fresh, they are highly irritant, being capable of producing a blister if bruised and laid on the skin; if applied to the abdomen, it is said that they will move the bowels. Taken inwardly, they act as a drastic purgative; sometimes as an emetic, and, in large doses, are likely to produce inflammation in the alimentary mucous membrane, and even death. From this root an alkaloid is extracted, called *Bryonin*, possessing its active properties in a concentrated degree. The term Bryony· is thought to be derived from *bryo*, to push or grow rapidly.

LAURELS.

Many of the Laurels are highly poisonous, on account of the quantity of prussic acid which they contain, and none more so than the *Laurus nobilis* of botanists, or Bay-tree. This is the true laurel of antiquity, with a wreath of which it was customary to crown successful competitors in the public games of the Greeks and Romans, and more recently those who gained the prizes offered for poetry and learning;

hence the title *Bacca laureatus*, or Bachelor, applied to university degrees. This laurel, though common enough in our shrubberies now, is a native of the shores of the Mediterranean. Its leaves are much used for flavouring custards; both these and the berries contain an aromatic and

stimulant oil; they were used by the old herbalists to relieve flatulency. They are seldom or ever now employed in this way, but sometimes are used to make a stimulant fomentation. The oil extracted from them is also made into a liniment; it is known in commerce as Laurel Oil.

The Common or Cherry Laurel (*Lauro-cerassus*) is a native of Asia Minor. This shrub also is not uncommon in our cultivated grounds; and its leaves are used for flavouring, like those of the last. They are more safe than the essence or oil of bitter almonds, but if used too largely may prove mischievous.

The Laurel Rose (*Nereum oleander*) is one of our most ornamental window plants. But it should be borne in mind that there is death in its very perfume; its emanations are so subtle that giddiness and fainting has resulted from inhaling them.

This, however, is not properly a Laurel, but belongs to the order *Apocynaceæ*, or Dog-berries. To show how impregnated is even the wood with poison, we may mention that during the Peninsular war a number of French soldiers went out foraging near Madrid, and returned laden with the fruits of their search. One of them cut a quantity of the boughs of this plant for skewers for the meat; they were stripped of their bark, and used for this purpose; and out of twelve who ate of the meat, seven died, and the rest were dangerously ill. We are also told of a child who ate a few of the lovely rose-like blossoms, and died in two days. The

Oleanders, of which this is one, like the Rhododendrons, are
nearly allied to the Laurels, and they are all more or less
poisonous.

GARDEN AND WINDOW CULTURE OF BRITISH WILD PLANTS.

No one can fail to admire well-hoed rows of kitchen garden
crops ; against the whole family of *weeds*, the grower of eat-
ables should wage incessant war. But in the flower-garden,
where there are no economical temptations to tread poetry
under foot, the process of weeding should be performed with
a little discrimination. The object of the flower-garden is
to present us at all seasons with the best assemblage of
beautiful and interesting forms, either of single plants or
well-massed groups. There are many enthusiastic flower-
growers, who will value nothing which is not expensive, and
who look with disdain on all common flowers. We must
admire the skill and the enthusiasm which such persons
usually manifest ; but, at the same time, we cannot but regret
the prejudice which blinds them to the virtues of the humbler
citizens of the flower world. I am passionately attached to
certain field favourites, and see in many of them beauties
which are not universally apparent. My attachment to the
old poets, and to old customs, and legends generally, has
given me a tendency to individualize field flowers, and to
regard them as a sort of personages akin to the fairies, so
that I have come at last to invest them with attributes of
even a higher order than those we are accustomed to associate
with the fantastic idealities of the old Saxon dreamers. The
result of this half childish frenzy is, that I have three times
spoilt a respectable garden by the introduction into it of
" all manner of weeds and wild rubbish."
My first experiments were made in a small garden at

Pentonville. In a close smoky district it is to be supposed my labours were sometimes unrewarded, but the rewards compensated, and none of my choice verbenas, hydrangeas, or cape heaths, ever gave me more pleasure than the first few groups of field plants that nodded good morning from the borders to the breakfast table. I then launched out among the rocks, with no danger to my life, but with some sore trials to my patience, and made some clinkers sparkle again with sprinklings of green and gold and ruby, so that my visitors were puzzled to know " what were those strange things in the rockwork ?" and I literally boiled over with joy to have a little bit of the wild woods close to my fireside. I will not weary the reader with an account of all the plants that played me false, of those that ran rampant and spoilt the flowering of adjacent exotics, of those that cost me miles of travel to procure, weeks of patient watching to rear, and of which I was utterly ashamed at last. Suffice it, that in the midst of smoke, a large number of our wild plants may be made to beautify the borders and parterres, the raised bank and the ornamental pond, while some are peculiarly fitted for growth in pots, to add variety to bowery windows.

The requisites in plants chosen for ornament, are grace or boldness of outline, distinct, cheerful, and profuse foliage, brilliancy and abundance of blossoms. Those which have rough leaves, straggling habits, or dull flowers, must continue weeds as ever, unless other reasons compel us to keep them under guardianship. Among the choicest wild plants for the border, are the hawkweed, the pimpernel, the speedwell, the yellow crocus, the purple lythrum, lychnis, tormentil, wood sorrel, and the bird's-foot trefoil. These are all plants of exquisite neatness and gaiety, easy of culture, and adaptable to almost any circumstances. The Hawkweeds, especially the pretty little mouse-ear hawkweed, make beautiful tufts, if grown between clumps of purple and white annuals. They require to be supported with short sticks and strips of bass, as they are apt to straggle in a procumbent growth. They bloom profusely. I have raised them from seed usually, obtaining it from dried specimens of the previous year; but I have often carried young plants home from the fields, and set them out in sandy soil, where they strike root at once, and bloom gaily from the end of June to the end of September. The Pimpernel (*Anagallis arvensis*) is truly a little gem; its gay coral-like eyes sleep, alas! too soon; stud its fresh heart-shaped leaves in profusion, and though it closes at mid-day, it teems with a thousand new eyes next morning. A fit companion for this, is the lovely Germander Speedwell (*Veronica chamædrys*), which puts out a similar abundance of bright azure eyes, which wink in the sunshine like fairies startled from a noon-day sleep. This pretty flower flourishes amazingly in a garden; a single plant soon increasing to a bed, covered with "bright azure eyes!" On one occasion, I had the good fortune to obtain a vast number of both these plants, from a packet professing to consist of *Anagallis indica*, and as the adulteration may have been an accident, and did me more good than harm, I shall not *Lancet* the seedsman who supplied me. I grouped the plants with patches of *Oxalis rosea, Lobelia gracilis*, and Bird's-foot Trefoil (*Lotus corniculatus*), in a little circular bed, on a grass-plot, under some standard roses, and the effect was charming in the extreme, the brilliant and almost unequalled gold hue of the bird's-foot giving the scene a gaiety quite fairy-like. The rosy oxalis above named I cannot too much commend to the lovers of minute elegancies. It may be found in the catalogue of Mr. Waite, of Holborn; otherwise I think it is somewhat scarce. The whole of the foregoing are best raised from seed; they frequently fall back after transplanting, and blossom before they make good root. · They should be sown where they are to stand, care being taken to dispose the colours well. Sandy or turfy loam suits them best, but they will not pine in the most barren rubbish.

The common Yellow Avens (*Geum urbanem*) is too fine a flower to be neglected by the lover of choice creations. It is very plentiful in the south of England, especially in Kent, Surrey, and Hampshire. The young plant must be taken up with as much mould as possible, and planted a little back in the border; it likes a generous soil, and if it is kept moderately dry, it has a sweet refreshing odour. The dried plants are frequently put into linen drawers in country places, to perfume the fruits of the housewife's industry. The sweet woodroof is another plant much used for this purpose, but it does not thrive in a garden, except far away among the nooks of hawthorn, where it rejoices in the damp shadow of trees, waiting to do service for wives proud of their skill in starching and ironing. Of all cool, homely, and respectable comforts, commend us to snow-white linen, washed in rain-water, dried on a lawn where blacks are strangers, and sweetened in the dark drawers by the benison of woodroof.

Our native Orchises are all suitable for borders, and highly ornamental if grown in large masses, the plants well crowded together, each cluster consisting of only one sort. They lose character if mixed. A very pretty way to grow orchises is to plant them in low rustic baskets, the plants closely packed together, one sort only in each basket, and the surface of the mould covered neatly with moss. Any one can make a rustic basket with a few seasoned loppings; and a pair filled with orchises have a choice and pleasing appearance on a grass-plot near a window, or on a broad gravel space. When the orchises go out of bloom they may be removed, and their place supplied with petunias, calceolarias, and other late-blooming showy plants. A stock of orchises must be obtained from the meadows; they cannot easily be raised from seed, nor can seed be readily procured.

The Purple Lythrum and the Willow Herb are both tall-growing plants. They are very gay, and have a pleasing effect if set back with white and yellow flowers before them.

The Ragged Robin is of similar character. Seeds of these
may be collected with ease from almost any hedge, in autumn,
and may be sown as soon as obtained in light sandy soil. If
kept till spring, they should be sown early in March, and in
the places where they are to stand; they may be transplanted
if it should be necessary, but they do not appear to bear the
process well.

Plants of this tall showy character have the best effect at
the back of a sloping bank, or the farther edge of a broad
border, where they are relieved by a jasmine or ivy wall, or
a mass of evergreens. Where there is sufficient space to
grow an abundance of tall showy wild plants, well mixed,
and sufficiently distant to soften their blendings, the effect
is truly delightful. A sloping bank may be thrown up at
the farther end of a garden, and fringed in one portion with
large dark stones, and in another with a gentle green de-
clivity of smooth turf, running down to a well-shaven plot,
interspersed with flower-bed or shrubs. One or two birches,
a willow and a maple, if there is sufficient room, should be
planted at the side, and they should be placed so that their
whole shadow may fall on the green slope. A rustic seat at
the base of the slope will improve the general appearance as
well as serve a useful purpose.

The rockwork should have but few light-coloured stones
amongst it, no shells of any kind, but be made up of large
dark and weather-worn masses. Its outline should be
neither too formal nor studiously fantastic, with easy slopes,
a few dark hollows, larger masses here and there upon the
upper ridge, and with a breadth of surface at top of six or
eight or ten feet if possible, or with only four feet where
space is scarce. In the country, such a bank might be built
where it would have a background of large trees and thick
umbrage; in town, a well-covered wall.

The upper borders of the front and sides of these banks
may be studded with bulbs of wild hyacinth, wild daffodil,
Poet's narcissus, lily of the valley, and single snowdrops for

the spring. These should be planted in large clumps on slopes, and a few of each stuck between the rocks in front, so as to continue the patches from above by a sort of fringe to the turf below. Alpine plants of all kinds may be planted advantageously in the crevices in front and on the upper edges. We should here find all our eleven species of wild stonecrop, or at least a few of the best known species, such as *Sedum telephium*, or the Orpine; the Yellow biting Stone-crop (*S. acre*), the White Orpine (*S. album*), and, if possible, that rare and beautiful variety *S. azureum*, whose blue blossoms shine out delightfully if well placed, and afford a good effect to the white pinks and yellows so prevalent among rock-plants. The Madwort (*Alyssum saxatile*), the Whiterock Wallcress (*Arabis saxatilis*), the Mountain Wall-flower (*Chiceranthus alpina*), the little Whitlow-grass, the Wall-pellitory, the Seathrift, the Woodroof, the Mountain Speedwell (*Veronica montana*), and the showy little plants which I have already advised make pretty borders. Here is a variety capable of much extension, composed entirely of beautiful and interesting plants; but there are a few of even choicer character than these, and I mention them separately. These are first the spider houseleek, a first-rate rock plant; the ivy-leaved toad-flax, the very gem of the smaller British plants; the common *Tormentilla*, or septfoil, the cinquefoil; the wild thyme, and the periwinkle. All these latter suit equally well for out-door and in-door grow-ing; their proper home is on the face of the rockwork, but if grown in pots in a compost of fine sand and leaf-mould, they attain a delightful luxuriance and a beauty not sur-passed by the choicest children of the greenhouse. All these plants are procurable at little trouble. The Toad-flax (*Lynaria cymbalaria*) may be met with on old walls and tombstones almost everywhere. It is a delicate creeper, furnished with abundance of minute ivy-shaped leaves of a dark green: its crimson tendrils have a waxen delicacy, and its blue blossoms, which appear from the middle of July to the end of September, are exquisitely formed after the ordinary model of a snapdragon. I obtain many wild plants from my own garden; for if weeding be performed with the help of botanic eyes, many choice things will be found to spring up spontaneously, even in the gardens about London. The toad-flax is impatient of disturbance, and, after being transplanted to its summer site, should be watered frequently and shaded from the sun.

The bank above should be planted with the glorious white snapdragon, the butterwort, the wild bugloss, the red rattle, the globe-flower (*Trollius Europœus*), orchises of all kinds, the rock rose (*Helianthemum vulgare*), hawkweeds, willow herbs of every variety, the wild lychnis, the wild rocket (*Erysimum alliaria*), and any varieties of mallow that can be obtained. The Common Mallow (*Malva sylvestris*) is a noble plant, and when nursed in the garden, its character improves considerably. The foliage acquires more neatness and the blooms become more abundant and of a darker tint. By preventing the formation of seed, its blooming is much prolonged. The Dwarf Mallow (*M. rotundifolia*) has a showy appearance, if brought near the edge of the raised border, and the fragrant Musk Mallow (*M. moschata*) is indispensable, as are also those noble plants, the common yarrow and meadow-sweet.

Farther back may be planted the lovely Musk thistle, the great Milk thistle, and the Cotton thistle (*Onopodum acanthium*). The mulleins are useful also in the background. The great mullein attains the height of five feet, and has a fine effect if its yellow club is backed by a mass of dark ivy. The hoary mullein and the little moth mullein are also useful —the latter being, however, of too dwarf a character to be set far back. The latter is frequent in Kent, but scarce elsewhere; but the other two abound in most parts of the country, and may be raised from seed collected from the plants when ripe.

A raised bank in a country garden may be made complete

by the addition of the harebell, the broom, the furze, the
ling, the sweet violet, the great bindweed, and the corn-
poppy; but none of these latter thrive in the neighbourhood of towns.

Even in the country, with every convenience, these last
named plants are not easily introduced, on account of their
slowness in taking root after transplanting. They may
however, be raised from seed, of which there is always an
abundance to be had in the proper season. Grown in sandy
soil, with abundance of sunlight, they are more cheerful and
ornamental in a garden than would be supposed, and only
need an occasional trimming to keep them from straggling
and in good shape.

Where there is a pond, several other very pretty wild
plants may be introduced with advantage; but as this opens
up another rather extensive subject, I will defer what I
have to say upon it until a future time.

Except when seed is wanted, make it a rule to clip off
shabby blooms, and even to thin out the bloom-buds of fine
plants. This method keeps up a better succession of flowers,
and many plants that in their native haunts ripen their
seeds and disappear, continue gay in the borders for several
weeks after the ordinary season of decay, while, if proper
care be bestowed upon them, their beauty far excels that of
their wild brethren. I sometimes have wild plants become
double under my care; I then cast them aside and replenish
my stock from the fields, for I think the charm is gone when
they alter character in this way, and begin apeing the
foreign greenhouse folks.

The best soil for wild plants generally is a mixture of
sharp sand and leaf mould, but generally speaking the
ordinary soil of a garden will do well enough. The Alpine
plants, and especially the little toad-flax, seem fond of lime,
and a little building rubbish would improve the soil for
them. If ferns are grown on a bank with flowering wild
plants, the same soil will suit all, and should be composed

of equal parts of sharp sand, leaf-mould or loam, pounded charcoal, and old building rubbish: a considerable sprinkling of broken bricks will improve it considerably. The Alpine plants on the face of the bank require watering very seldom, but ferns should be watered, in dry weather, twice every day.

I mention little details of this kind, in the hope of stirring up a love for these simple things among those who have a tender regard for plants generally. I should like to see the abolition of that prejudice which leads us to twist our ideas of taste into conformity with every petty conventionality, and which blinds us to the beauty of such objects as are common and cheap. Let us welcome whatever of the beautiful the world affords us; but let not the children of our native soil be utterly thrust aside by their less hardy exotic compeers.

Such is the garland of flowers which we have culled in all seasons, and blended with red berries and yellow leaves in autumn. Very pleasant to us has been the gathering of them: and sweet is the remembrance of our rambles through meadows, and by streams, on breezy commons, and in woods where the *Linnæa borealis* lifts up her head, and diffuses a pleasant fragrance. Gusty winds are now abroad, and snow storms are careering across the fields; the heavens are covered with clouds, and men feel the icy blast that warns of increasing cold; but the time will come when all leafless branches shall be re-clothed with verdure, and flowers again peep forth. When, therefore, you next visit your favourite haunts, look for the familiar faces of such flowers as we have herein selected for you, and remember the associations connected with them.

London: Printed by H. Tuck, New Street, Cloth Fair.